MADAME PRESIDENT 1901-1905

Nellie Fairbanks, Path Finder To Politics
for American Women

by

Lucy Jane King

authorHOUSE®

AuthorHouse™
1663 Liberty Drive, Suite 200
Bloomington, IN 47403
www.authorhouse.com
Phone: 1-800-839-8640

First published by AuthorHouse   4/29/2008

ISBN: 978-1-4343-8593-2 (sc)
ISBN: 978-1-4343-8594-9 (hc)

Library of Congress Control Number: 2008927920

Printed in the United States of America
Bloomington, Indiana

This book is printed on acid-free paper.

Dedication

To the memory of my parents.

There would have been no women's rights movement in the United States if middle-class women had not been so well-behaved.

Laurel Thatcher Ulrich

Table of Contents

Preface — xi

Chapter One　　　Striving to Make the Country Better......................1

Chapter Two　　　Developing and Making Decisions......................11

Chapter Three　　Speaking Out................................17

Chapter Four　　　Roles of a Woman................................25

Chapter Five　　　Destined to Be a Leader................................41

Chapter Six　　　Frontiers................................53

Chapter Seven　　Political Foremothers................................63

Chapter Eight　　　Reins of Government Well in Hand......................75

Chapter Nine　　　Building a National Audience......................87

Chapter Ten　　　Politics Is Good Fun................................101

Chapter Eleven　　Building a Stately Mansion................................111

Chapter Twelve　　Memorial to the Past, Incentive for the Future...121

Chapter Thirteen　Wife of the Vice President................................139

Chapter Fourteen　So Many Americans Scattered Over the Earth....155

Chapter Fifteen　　Farewell Address................................169

Chapter Sixteen　　Final Years................................179

Epilogue — 185

Notes — 187

Selected Bibliography — 221

List of Illustrations — 225

Acknowledgements — 229

Preface

A new century, a controversial war conceived as response to a terrorist threat from a foreign country, political fights between conservatives and liberals, and arguments about the role of women in politics: the year was 1901. The United States had just fought the Spanish-American War resulting from alleged Spanish involvement in the explosion of an American battleship. A country that had elected conservative president William McKinley was not only shocked by his assassination by an anarchist gunman with a foreign name but also uncertain about what changes would occur with the new progressive president Theodore Roosevelt. There were arguments about whether or not women should even be allowed to vote, much less to hold office.

Yet there was a national women's organization at the time that considered the office of their president to be the highest office for women in America—the female equivalent of president of the United States.[1] The Daughters of the American Revolution held political conventions reported in national media, elected national as well as state and local officers, and had a national Congress. This book is about the woman they elected president in 1901, Cornelia Cole Fairbanks. Mrs. Fairbanks was middle class, well behaved, and a strong supporter of women's rights.

It would be just over a century before a woman could credibly campaign to be president of the United States in a major political party. She would have more public acceptance than her many forgotten predecessors,[2] but almost a third of the electorate still thought the country was not ready for a woman president.[3] Even so, by 2008, a woman was Speaker of the House of Representatives; sixteen women were U.S. senators; and there were seventy-four women members of the House. Nine women were governors of states. They included both Democrats and Republicans.[4] Many of these women were wives and daughters of politicians, as was Mrs. Fairbanks. In the twenty-first century, women no longer have to depend on male relatives' positions to be successful in politics. Neither did Mrs. Fairbanks. Although accused of gaining prominence solely because her husband was a United States senator, she earned the office on her own merits.

In Mrs. Fairbanks's day, some women had been working actively for voting rights since the mid-nineteenth century, facing verbal and often physical abuse. Others were assuming new roles delicately but influentially. They, too, formed one of the links between nineteenth-century women's organizations and twenty-first-century women elected to state and national office.

Marriage and politics continue to be related in complex ways for women. Husbands of female politicians inevitably impact campaigns of women seeking office—for better or for worse. Wives of male politicians are more likely, now, to be accepted as professional women, competent in their own right and not just as subjects for family photo opportunities. Cornelia Fairbanks read law and assisted her husband in his practice. She achieved fame as a charming hostess in Washington, D.C., and was very much involved in his political campaigns.

Her husband, Charles Warren Fairbanks, was elected Theodore Roosevelt's vice president. He described his wife as "a great woman … democratic in manner and thought; a scholar and a speaker of attractive and persuasive power; a friend and wise counselor of the young … eager to exalt her own sex."[5] She was seen by a woman of her day as "a striking and beautiful example … of the development of the modern woman."[6] She believed that women should vote and take an active part in politics.[7]

A century ago, as the clamor for votes for women was reaching its peak, Mrs. Fairbanks was one of the best known women in the United States[8] and was considered "about as clever a politician as her husband."[9] Active on the national board of the General Federation of Women's Clubs, "she touched the lives of a very large number of women ... she was a woman of whom all women could be proud."[10] She was a complex woman—devoted to family and home, but not to domesticity; feminine, yet a suffragist and proponent of the rights of women.[11] Her career in the public eye contributed positively and powerfully to attitudes about woman suffrage and women in public office. She was a pathfinder for what was to come in the twentieth and twenty-first centuries.

Chapter One

STRIVING TO MAKE THE COUNTRY BETTER

In order to understand fully the still changing roles of women in politics in the early twenty-first century, it is useful to explore the lives of those who were transforming women's roles at the beginning of the twentieth century and the social trends in the nineteenth century that had led to their status. Various kinds of seeds had been planted. Tilling the soil was difficult. There were good years and bad.

Nineteenth-century proto-feminists were as diverse as their twentieth-century feminist successors. They were under social pressure to remain "feminine," dutiful wives and mothers, moral arbiters influencing society only from the home as they educated their children in good citizenship. Women who strayed from that stereotype were not treated well. Some behaved heroically in the presence of verbal and even physical abuse as they spoke out in public for women's rights. Suffragists, particularly, stood out as reformers—in the eyes of some, dangerously so.

In what would become important for women in politics, westward expansion was a major trend in nineteenth-century America. Early in the century, the "Old Northwest Territories" were settled— grandparents of Cornelia Cole Fairbanks were among the settlers—and soon gained statehood in what would become the Midwest. Further westward expansion as the century progressed gave new freedom to women, especially white women. "Many younger women found rigid gender conventions relaxed when their small numbers in a newly settled region required that the talents of every individual be exploited regardless of age, gender, and status."[1] The frontier was difficult, but it had its rewards for many.

African-American women were taken, or sold, west before the Civil War and, like their men, went west to new freedom after the war. Native American women were important on the frontier. Some of them held leadership roles in their tribes. Often, Mexican women had more property rights than white women as the Southwest became settled. Both Native Americans and Mexican Americans suffered great losses, but many survived the rigors. Granddaughters and great-granddaughters of minority women became successful in the twentieth century, including in politics. After the Civil War, the influx of immigrants from Europe fueled further expansion. Many of the Western states adopted woman suffrage long before Eastern states.[2] A woman in Denver in the 1890s praised her state as a "dwelling place where free speech would not be denied [women] of all nationalities."[3]

In the more conservative maturing frontier of mid-America, many women worked behind the scenes, quietly redefining their roles to fit within what was acceptable in traditional views of women's roles. At the same time, they were advancing the status of women. They were devoted wives and mothers and ardent clubwomen, and they were subtly promoting the political rights of women. Less confrontational pursuits attracted more women to these endeavors than to the barricades of overt protest, and they had influence in ways those openly nonconformist individuals could not have.[4] All these differing women contributed to twentieth-century feminism and political participation.

Some women fit the stereotypes when they were young and moved into public, more controversial activities as they grew older. The four founders of the Daughters of the American Revolution provide examples of changing roles throughout life. Mary Smith Lockwood, the widow of a Civil War Union soldier, became an author and suffragist. Eugenia Washington had to support her disabled father after her mother died when Eugenia was nineteen. She worked for the post office in Washington, D.C., and never married. Mary Desha was also an unmarried federal government employee. She had studied at what is now the University of Kentucky, founded a private school with her mother, and taught in the territory of Alaska. After the death of her husband, Ellen Hardin Walworth ran a boarding day school in New York City and later earned a law degree. She was licensed to practice law in both New York and the District of Columbia.[5]

In April of 1890, the Sons of the American Revolution, descendants of Revolutionary War veterans, voted to exclude women, "galvanizing a force as determined as that which fought for American independence."[6] A subsequent series of meetings of the women in Washington, D.C., led to the founding of the Daughters of the American Revolution (DAR) in October of 1890. William McDowell, one of the founders of the Sons of the American Revolution whose female ancestor had been a brave patriot, supported them.[7]

Whatever one thought of hearth and home and the roles of women therein, a family could no longer supply all its needs as the nineteenth century wore on. The industrial revolution was moving production of household items from home to factory. Both men and women were employed in factory work. Wage differentials favored men, although the work was grueling for all and had few, if any, benefits such as health insurance or guarantees of safe workplaces. Organizations of workers developed to remedy these situations. Owners of corporations and businesses fared much better. A new middle class was growing and prospering. They formed their own organizations and clubs. "Charley" and "Nellie" Fairbanks were very much a part of the new, prosperous middle class. Religion, especially Protestant Christianity, was important in nineteenth-century America. Early in the century, the Second Great Awakening had inspired women to support missionary work both at home and abroad. Religious fervor also promoted benevolent societies to help the poor and working people. Benevolence was respectable and womanly. Later in the century, as many Protestant churches became more mainstream, women continued to be active in women's societies in churches, an approved activity for a lady. Jewish women formed benevolent societies, especially addressing helping children. Sometimes they and their Christian neighbors joined together in such efforts. Catholic nuns provided strong role models of women as teachers and nurses.[8]

Historian Anne Firor Scott cautioned that we should not dismiss efforts to save people from sin or to bring them to Jesus as purely self-righteous. These were enormously energizing for nineteenth-century women. We might view this as condescension; in the nineteenth century, such religious activity was perceived positively. Because their language sounds so excessive now, we might well fail to understand just how strong-minded many of these women were.[9] Nellie Fairbanks supported missionary work and was seen by her friends as deeply spiritual, not self-righteous.

Although early in the century women's education was seen as preparation for educating their own children in the home, after the Civil War, public education became more prevalent and included both boys and girls. There were efforts to provide education for former slaves. In the public sector, they were often segregated under the cynical rubric "separate but equal." The first generation of women to graduate from female colleges around the time of the Civil War or soon after had expectations of additional duties to society at large.[10] "Nellie" Cole was in this generation of graduates and accepted additional duties in her community after her marriage to Charles Fairbanks.

As the century progressed, women read more. The development of the novel as a literary form provided insights into the lives of women protagonists. Domestic novels promoted the idea that homemakers could make a difference, as had Harriet Beecher Stowe's *Uncle Tom's Cabin*, in which housewives helped escaping slaves.[11]

Women had gained more independence during the Civil War. Although the passage of black women from slavery to at least nominal freedom was more obvious, white women on both sides had learned to carry increasing burdens on the home front and in supporting the troops. Neither black nor white women gained the vote nationally, but they had seen that remarkable social change was possible.[12] They also saw that there was still more work to be done to bring about changes not yet completed. Black men were the granted the right to vote—at least on paper—in 1870, women not until 1920.

The Progressive Era was an era of Jim Crow.[13] There was segregation even in women's clubs. Organizations of women of color and white women's clubs—both active and both including educated, middle-class, civic-minded, patriotic women—were often separate. Many national women's organizations were either all black or all white in membership or at least segregated in terms of membership in particular clubs. Members of the General Federation of Women's Clubs at the turn of the twentieth century voted not to accept the representative from a Massachusetts black women's club even though the executive committee of the Federation had voted to accept her.[14] Mrs. Fairbanks was elected to the national board of the Federation that same year and undoubtedly agreed with admission of the black delegate. Her father had been involved in the Underground Railroad in Ohio for escaping slaves and was a supporter of Abraham Lincoln. Her husband had first become prominent in national politics at the Republican National Convention in 1896, which seated Negro delegates from some of the former slave states. In recent elections, those states had been carried by Republicans for the first time since Reconstruction.[15] In later speeches in the South, Charles Fairbanks spoke of freedom for all. Black women's clubs formed their own societies, such as the National Association of Colored Women, organized in 1896. Like white women's clubs, they used "the language of domesticity and of their responsibility as women" to address relevant issues.[16] Uplift of their race was a crucial issue, as well as women's rights. Many of them would become involved in organizing the National Association for the Advancement of Colored People in 1909 and other forerunners of the mid-twentieth-century civil rights movement.[17]

Discussion of civil rights for African-Americans and women's rights sometimes led to heated debates like one between women's rights pioneer Elizabeth Cady Stanton and abolitionist Frederick Douglass at a meeting in New York City in 1869. In reporting this and subsequent events, journalist Mark Leibovich pointed out that "the civil rights movement and the women's movement have a long, complicated history dating back to abolitionism and the origins of modern feminism."[18] The Daughters of the American Revolution at the time of Mrs. Fairbanks's presidency still had sufficient southern and other members whose views kept it from embracing black members. Even in 1939, renowned black opera singer Marion Anderson was refused the right to sing at the DAR Constitution Hall. First Lady Eleanor Roosevelt resigned her membership and arranged for Ms. Anderson to sing on the steps of the Lincoln Memorial,[19] almost thirty years before the Rev. Martin Luther King would give his "I Have a Dream" speech at that same location. The Daughters changed later in the twentieth century. African-American descendents of Revolutionary War soldiers are now members, and exhibits at the national museum honor black patriots.[20]

Women's literary clubs in the last decades of the century allowed individuals to meet with one another, present book reports, and discuss their reading. Members of these clubs not only educated themselves about "women's" topics like literature and history but also about subjects considered more "masculine"—politics and government. Discussions held in the context of coffee or tea and dessert in a woman's attractively furnished, genteel parlor or in the rooms of one of the newly constructed women's club buildings seemed less threatening to the public than street marches demanding votes. Many clubs moved, over time, from self improvement, to community improvement, to improvement of the nation through political action.[21]Concern with art, beauty, and community improvement was acceptable as womanly. Women became supporters of music societies, art museums, and garden clubs. These activities often required cooperation with local government authorities in the construction of parks and buildings for cultural activities. Patriotism and nationalism became important as the country was beginning to heal the wounds of civil war and to deal with new waves of immigrants from many countries. The Spanish-American War at the end of the century furthered nationalism, overseas expansion, and concern for bringing American democracy to other countries. Patriotic fervor was womanly as long as it was confined to helping the troops with food, supplies, and medical care, which women did again during the Spanish-American War at the end of the century as they had done earlier on both sides of the Civil War.

Because competition between political parties was becoming fiercer in the last quarter of the nineteenth century, women's aid to them became more important. Women formed clubs supporting political parties, part of a middle-class reform movement by both men and women to clean up the boisterous gatherings and hard-drinking behavior associated with campaigns and elections in the earlier days of the century.[22] Women like Mrs. Fairbanks who were wives of prominent politicians could provide behind-the-scenes influence on their husbands' more public work as had always been women's role. Now, with more education, they were more often advisors as well as comforters. During the last decade or so of the nineteenth century and into the twentieth, women's clubs began to form national organizations, prominent among them the General Federation of Women's Clubs that included a wide variety of local and state organizations. Others were much more specialized, like the Daughters of the American Revolution, the Women's Christian Temperance Union, the National Woman Suffrage Association, the Working Women's Association, the National Congress of Mothers, the Women's Auxiliary of the Outdoor Art and Park Improvement Association, the National Household Economics Association, and on and on, almost ad infinitum.[23]

Recent scholarship has seen these national groups as the first blossoming of women's organizations, the second being in the 1960s and 1970s with civil rights struggles, anti-war movements, and efforts to obtain an Equal Rights Amendment to the U.S. Constitution. These times of rapid growth have occurred at times of significant social change. In the 1890s and early 1900s, women were being mobilized from their homes where they were wives and mothers into the public sphere where they played important roles in organizations often associated with political action.[24] As a result, women were learning to balance busy schedules not only in the home as they had always done, but also in new projects outside the home. Working for causes beneficial to the community gave women the opportunity to learn public speaking and methods of advertising their projects and raising money. Fund-raising and management necessitated gaining knowledge of business principles. Directing the work of others led to expanding administrative skills already known to managers of busy households. Womanly activities were being used as a political force to impact many areas of society.

Women's associations provided careers—"careers from which the income was psychic rather than material. In their own groups women learned to be professionals before the traditional professions were open to them, and developed a recognizable female style of professional behavior that relied heavily on cooperation."[25]

Nellie Fairbanks accrued just such nonmaterial career benefits as a leader in a national women's organization and developed a style that was professional and relied on cooperation. She began her influence on politics at home, advising her husband about his law practice and about entry into politics in the 1880s. She initiated her women's club work by organizing the first all-women's literary club in Indianapolis in her home in 1885 while her children were still small. The club's discussion topics included current events. She was on the board of a group that planned and supervised construction of a building for meetings of this and many other local women's groups.

In a reform movement, she was appointed to the State Board of Charities. Then, her husband's election to the Senate of the United States and her national office in the Daughters of the American Revolution (DAR) led to her greatest opportunity to further the rights of "her own sex which she was eager to exalt."[26]

As a leader of the DAR at the turn of the twentieth century, she summed up for a journalist the history and role of clubwomen: "The club woman of today, about which there is so much discussion, contrary to the generally accepted opinion, is not a new product. She dates from the very foundation of [American] society, and her influence has been felt in every age.

"Women of Colonial times had their clubs and concerned themselves with public questions, on a much smaller scale, to be sure, than the influential clubs of today, because they had not the advantages of a liberal education and their clubs were mostly tea parties. Nevertheless, club women are not a recent discovery.

"As the women of the Revolution worked untiringly to help save the country in time of war, so the modern club woman is striving to make it better, morally and intellectually, in peace.

"The society which I have the honor to represent counts among its members some of the ablest club women in America. I am always proud to remember that club women are ever to be found wielding their great influence for good. Politics and monetary considerations do not weigh with a club woman against the dictates of her conscience. Therefore, I say, the club woman is a desirable adjunct to the body politic.

"American men have been of the greatest assistance in developing the modern club woman. They respect her opinions in the matter of civic problems, and often invite her cooperation. The greater advantages of education have increased the list of club members, but the spirit is the same as that of America's earlier days. 'Upward and onward' is their motto. Courageously helpful in war, courage is not less necessary in peace as most any prominent club woman of today can testify."[27]

Chapter Two

Developing and Making Decisions

Cornelia Cole Fairbanks's professional and political style began to develop very early in her life—a life typical of middle-class nineteenth-century American women in many ways. Some paths opened for her; others were closed. She made choices as she found her way. Many fathers in the 1860s, or even much later, would not have thought that way, but Judge Philander B. Cole of Marysville, Ohio, wanted his three daughters as well as his three sons to attend college. As a young man, P. B. Cole had attended college for a year at the school that would become Dennison University, in Granville, Ohio; but illness and, especially, lack of funds sent him back to Marysville, where for a time, he taught school. As always, he continued to read widely. He studied law with another lawyer, as did many Midwestern lawyers then, and entered politics as a successful candidate of the Whig Party for prosecuting attorney in 1838. He and his law mentor started a newspaper. He served on the Board of Education and on the Library Board of Union County. His children would grow and mature in an environment nourished by literature, law, politics, and newspaper publishing.

Dorothy B. ("Dollie") Witter was the daughter of the third man to be sheriff of Union County, of which Marysville was the county seat.

She and P. B. Cole were married there in 1839. Both their families had been among the early settlers of Union County in the first and second decades of the nineteenth century. Their three sons, after graduating from college, became lawyers like their father. Ulysses, a graduate of Kenyon College in 1862, served in the Union Army in the Civil War and then studied law at Harvard and with his father. James, a West Point graduate in 1866, later studied and practiced law in Marysville. Edward, a graduate of Ohio Wesleyan University in 1874, studied and practiced law in Marysville with his father. Cornelia ("Nellie") Cole graduated from Ohio Wesleyan Female College in 1872. Jessie graduated from Western Female Seminary in Oxford, Ohio, and Dollie from Ohio Wesleyan Female College and Cincinnati College of Music.[1] By 1900, 60 percent of American high school graduates were women; more than 30 percent of college students were women; and women received almost 20 percent of the bachelor's degrees awarded annually.[2] By another estimate, the opening of coeducational federal land grant colleges in the Midwest and western United States and the founding of female colleges in the East in the last half of the nineteenth century meant that women made up approximately 40 percent of the total number of college graduates at the end of the century.[3] Nellie Cole her sisters attained that goal a quarter century earlier. They were already ahead of their time.

Nellie, the eldest daughter of P. B. and Dollie Cole, was actively athletic, riding a horse with her brother Edward around Marysville and the nearby fields and woods of the gently rolling Ohio countryside where corn and wheat flourished and cattle and sheep grazed. She loved the outdoors and most of all flowers. Gardening would become one of her passions. Judge Cole and Nellie shared literary tastes and often discussed their reading. "She had a very retentive memory, quick perception, and an intense desire to learn," and was "always a lover of literature and read unceasingly." In common schools in Marysville, she became recognized as a charming and popular young lady, an outstanding scholar, and an inspiring public speaker. As a girl, she joined the Presbyterian Church, was active in Sunday school, and was as widely read in the Bible as in history and literature.[4] Her local church, when begun in the 1820s, had been on the frontier and like other such churches was visited by missionaries until it had sufficient parishioners to hire its own minister.[5] Nellie would later become interested in missionary work on other frontiers.

She became captivated by patriotism and by politics. Throughout her childhood, she had heard the conversations of her parents and older brothers, their friends, and political colleagues. Her father served in the Ohio State Legislature and the Ohio Senate. He was then elected judge of the Court of Common Pleas in Union County. Like many other Northern members of the Whig Party, P. B. Cole became a member of the new Republican Party founded in 1854. He had participated in the underground railroad for escaping slaves, worked enthusiastically for the election of Abraham Lincoln in 1860, and supported Lincoln again as a delegate to the Republican National Convention in 1864.[6] Ohio, a Northern state, was across the Ohio River from border state Kentucky. Harriet Beecher Stowe's antislavery book *Uncle Tom's Cabin* had been written in Cincinnati to the southwest of Marysville. Union General Ulysses S. Grant had been born to the south in Point Pleasant, Ohio, along the Ohio River. Ohio was raided by Kentucky Confederate General Morgan's raiders during the Civil War, when Nellie was a young adolescent and her elder two brothers were in the military.

In the fall of 1862 when Nellie was in her early teens, invasion of Cincinnati, a little more than a hundred miles away from Marysville as the crow flies, was threatened by Confederates forces. The governor of Ohio sent out a call for help throughout southwestern Ohio communities. Within a few hours, thousands poured into the city. Within three days, there were several thousand armed men prepared to counterattack any invasion. Confederate forces threatened the city for eight days, but made no overt move against it. The Ohio "Squirrel Hunters" were sharp-shooters. Confederate soldiers decided against attacking Cincinnati and withdrew. Union County furnished fifteen officers and eighty privates to the Yankee defenders.[7] Patriotism was in the air. Nellie Cole, in a politically active family during a war that came so close to home, was aware of changes in the country and changing roles of women on the home front. After the war, gradually, patriotic feelings about the Founding Fathers of America, whom all the country respected, would begin to serve toward uniting North and South. The new nationalism would also be associated not only with westward expansion of the United States but also, at the end of the century, with overseas expansion that Nellie would later observe first-hand.

Like other adolescents, Cornelia Cole began to define herself. She adopted the nickname the family had given her, "Nellie," and thereafter would be known to family and close friends by that name. She apparently shaved some years off her age in late adolescence, possibly to appear the same age as her classmates when she returned to Ohio Wesleyan Female College after a time at home in Marysville.[8] Following early training at the Academy of the Reverend James Smith and later at the public Union High School in Marysville, she went to the Young Ladies Seminary in Granville, Ohio. For her sophomore year, 1867–68, she attended Ohio Wesleyan Female College in Delaware, Ohio. She then lived at home in Marysville.[9] Nellie's time at home was a time of decision-making for a young woman—even one from a family like hers—whose options were limited. While in Marysville, she was a substitute teacher for a friend who was ill. Although she was a successful teacher and saw education of the young as an important role, she chose not to continue in that profession.[10] She might have participated in P. B. Cole's law practice, perhaps performing some of the tasks a legal secretary or paralegal would do today. Her father engaged in a busy general practice of law. Her eldest brother, Ulysses, practiced law with their father in 1866, but after a year, moved to Indiana. Brothers James and Edward would join the practice in the early 1870s.[11] To become a lawyer and join her father in practice as her brothers did would have been well nigh impossible for a young lady. It was only in 1870 that the first woman graduated from an American law school, in Chicago.[12]

Teaching seemed not to be the way for Nellie Cole; law couldn't be at the time. Her path would become more visible when she returned to Ohio Wesleyan Female College.

Chapter Three

SPEAKING OUT

At Ohio Wesleyan Female College, Nellie Cole was active in the Clionian Literary Club. Appropriately, "Light, More Light" was the motto of the club.[1] She would see the way to her future at Ohio Wesleyan.

Inspiring public speaking would become one of her most valuable talents. Women had generally not been allowed to speak publicly in the early nineteenth century. For example, when Dorothea Dix wanted to present to the United States Congress her plea for the reform of institutions for patients with psychiatric disorders, she turned to her neighbor and friend, Senator John Adams Dix (no relation). He presented her memorial on June 27, 1848, "emphasizing that as a lady she hesitated to address Congress, and he read the dramatic closing passages of her petition to his colleagues and the crowded gallery."[2] As women began to be depicted in novels and other writing as speaking out, and as they actually began to speak in public, their voices made major contributions to public discourse. Caroline Field Levander has demonstrated convincingly that the tone of women's speaking, as opposed to the speech of men, was an element of cultural change in the nineteenth century.[3] Public speaking opened up the first pathway for

Nellie Cole and had obvious implications, later, for women in politics. At the final program in the spring of 1872 given for the public by the Clionian Society, Nellie delivered a speech of which the *Delaware (Ohio) Herald* reported: "The oration of Miss Nellie Cole was beyond doubt the finest one of the evening. The first paragraph which follows is a fair example of the entire oration:

'We read in legendary lore that Aphrodite, the fairest of the divinities, sprung from the sea foam in the perfection of her intellect, power, and beauty. So Patriotism, that grandest mainspring of disinterested human action, springs from the emergency of the hour in all of the strength of its heaven-bestowed endowments of beauty, endurance, and self-sacrifice.'"[4]

She saw patriotism as disinterested and heaven-bestowed, not selfish or xenophobic, especially in view of the recent emergency of the hour, a massive Civil War that had come close to home for her. Heaven, itself, had bestowed patriotism with endurance and self-sacrifice—a perspective that would guide her most important public work in the future.

In 1872, Miss Cole gave a speech at commencement ceremonies for the female college on "Phases of Religion." The *Ohio State Journal* noted, "Miss Cole's oration on 'Phases of Religion' was remarkable for the evidence it gave of extensive reading and maturity of thought. She seemed as much at home with the Grecian gods and philosophers as girls of her apparent age usually are with Dickens or Bronte."[5] Knowledge and acceptance of various philosophical and religious views, as well as her own deep spirituality, would also characterize her perspective in the future. In her senior year, she worked with one of the editors of the *Western Collegian*, Charley Fairbanks. She was an associate editor, contributing news and comments from the sister college to the eight-page, semi-monthly college paper in 1871–72. Some discussions in the paper that year addressed the issue of whether or not women and men should be enrolled in the same colleges. Many students favored uniting the two colleges of Ohio Wesleyan into one institution; others did not.[6] Union of the colleges took place in 1877, five years after Nellie and Charley graduated from their separate colleges. By that time, over four hundred young women, including Cornelia Cole, had graduated from Ohio Wesleyan Female College.[7] Mr. Charles Fairbanks spoke at commencement week ceremonies at Ohio Wesleyan University on "Public Sentiment" and debated at one of the men's college societies on "Which exert the greatest influence in our country, the Lawyers, the Clergy, or the Businessmen?"[8] He would become both a lawyer and a businessman, and was active in his church as a layman.

Charles Warren Fairbanks was born and raised on a farm near Unionville, in the southern part of Union County, Ohio.[9] He would become one of the last American politicians to claim a log cabin birthright—or at least birth in a farmhouse partly constructed of logs. Nellie Cole had grown up in Marysville, the county seat of Union County. They did not meet until they went to college in nearby Delaware, Ohio, in Delaware County. It is quite possible that some of their relatives had met as Union County was being settled earlier in the century or when business or legal matters took some of the Fairbanks family to Marysville. In the mid-nineteenth century, that journey through the county required considerably more time and effort than the twenty-minute drive of today. "Romance throve at Delaware. It was there ... that [President] Rutherford B. Hayes met and became engaged to Lucy Webb, and it was there that Charles Warren Fairbanks, later vice president, met his wife-to-be, Cornelia Cole."[10] Later newspaper articles about Mrs. Fairbanks after her husband became nationally prominent often described their college romance in flowery terms. Their daughter Adelaide Fairbanks indicated in an interview years later that their relationship in college had not been social and certainly not romantic.[11]College romance in the 1870s was far different than the easy socializing on campuses today. Indeed, many colleges accepted only male or only female students or, like Ohio Wesleyan, had separate colleges for each. In a Methodist institution like Ohio Wesleyan, and in most other American colleges of the day, frequent social interaction among male and female students was not usually possible. When it occurred, it was carefully chaperoned.

Although both were in the small town of Delaware, Ohio, Ohio Wesleyan University and Ohio Wesleyan Female College were located many blocks apart. Young ladies at the female college rarely, if ever, were allowed to leave campus without a chaperone. The wife of the president of the female college served as "preceptress" for the women in the college dormitory rooms. By the 1870s when Charley and Nellie were there, the rigid separation of the men from Ohio Wesleyan and the women from Ohio Wesleyan Female College was changing—a little. The Saturday night reception was instituted at the female college in 1870: A young lady would send a very proper invitation for the reception to a young gentleman. The young man fortunate enough to receive the invitation would write a formal note in response. His note was opened by the preceptress. If she approved, the young lady was given permission to answer in the affirmative. On the Saturday evening of the reception to which they had been invited, the young gentlemen appeared in their Prince Albert coats, sent up their calling cards to the young ladies in the dormitory floor, and awaited their hostesses. Their choices of activities were either to sit in two adjoining chairs along with all the other couples in the reception room or to promenade the hall. Young men had to leave promptly at 8:30 p.m. No exceptions were allowed by the preceptress.[12]

If Nellie Cole, as an associate editor from the female college, delivered her news reports and commentaries in person to Editor Charley Fairbanks at the *Western Collegian*, their meetings would likely have been fairly brief and rather well supervised. In the nineteenth century, they would not have spent hours together, long into the night, among other college men and women putting together a campus newspaper, as would students later in the twentieth century. Ohio Wesleyan had been in existence less than three decades when Charley attended. The oldest building, Elliot Hall, had been built in 1833 as a resort hotel near mineral springs. When it suffered financial reverses, the Reverend Charles Elliott convinced the Methodist Church in 1841 to buy the property for a college, and worked to raise necessary funds for the purchase.[13] Thomson Chapel was built in 1853. Sturges Library was built later in the 1850s. President Thomson of the college toured Europe in order to collect 3,000 books for the library, making it one of the best college libraries in the United States at the time.[14] Two acres of attractive plantings formed a center for the three buildings—the college Charlie Fairbanks entered in 1868.

In Charles's sophomore year, the faculty suspended two students who had prepared, as a joke, a mock program for a debate between two men's societies. Charles defended them in a stirring address to a student protest meeting, invoking their rights under the United States Constitution. Students agreed with him, but he had hazarded official condemnation. He would have been sent home had not the acting president, Professor L. D. McCabe, come to his defense. "After that hour, Fairbanks was the most popular man in the university."[15] It is understandable that the Reverend Doctor McCabe would later be asked to perform the marriage ceremony for Charles and Nellie.

The female college began in the home of William Little, who had contributed generously when the original building for Ohio Wesleyan was bought. When one hundred girls enrolled in the first year, a wooden structure was built nearby to house them.[16] Mary Monnett came to the female college in 1854. In 1857, she donated money to complete construction of a more adequate building, Monnett Hall. In 1864, a new addition gave more dormitory space, a basement dining hall, two society halls, and a chapel. Although the enrollment of Ohio Wesleyan University was decimated by the Civil War as young men went off to join the Union Army, the female college was able to continue educating women—enrollment in 1862, just a few years before Nellie entered, was over 200 students.[17] At "Monnett Hall," Nellie "took high rank as a brilliant scholar, and had all of her fellow students for friends. Without effort she became one of the most popular girls in school."[18] After college, Nellie lived at home again in Marysville, as did her sisters between college graduation and marriage, and as did any other young lady of the time who was not married. Charles was a reporter for the Western Associated Press, managed by his mother's brother William Henry Smith. He worked in Pittsburgh and in Cleveland, where he completed law school and passed the Ohio Bar Examination in 1874.[19]

Some time after graduation from Ohio Wesleyan, Charles and Nellie met at a party, became reacquainted, and began courting according to the custom of their day.[20]

It is not surprising that he was attracted to a strong, accomplished young woman. His mother, Mary Adelaide Smith Fairbanks, was a "woman of tireless energy … the family's guiding force … deeply religious and passionately dedicated to the temperance movement … [she] had a strong will, quick apprehension, and considerable executive ability."[21]

No doubt the Coles were happy for their daughter to be courted by an up-and-coming, hard-working, church-attending young lawyer originally from Union County. Mr. and Mrs. Fairbanks likely were happy, too, that their son Charles was courting Judge Cole's daughter.

The *Akron (Ohio) Daily Beacon* reported on October 6, 1874, "Marysville society is in a glow this evening in attendance at the marriage of Mr. Charles W. Fairbanks, attorney of the Indianapolis, Bloomington, and Western Railroad, and Miss Nellie Cole."[22] The ceremony took place in the Presbyterian Church. They were married by the Rev. Dr. McCabe. The *Marysville Tribune* noted, "The church was well filled upon this occasion with the friends of the parties. The ceremony being over, a large party embracing several hundred of our citizens assembled at Judge Cole's residence to congratulate the bride and groom in their new relation, and to partake of a rich bounty for the occasion … the bridal party left on the train for Chicago, and from thence to Indianapolis, their future home. Our best wishes accompany our friends."[23]

Chapter Four

ROLES OF A WOMAN

The families of both Charles and Nellie Fairbanks had originally ventured from Britain or Holland in the seventeenth century to colonies in America and had gradually moved westward with the frontier. Charles and Nellie continued the typical nineteenth-century American westward journey. After marriage, they moved to a growing metropolis farther west—industrializing Indianapolis, fast becoming a regional railroad center.

White Anglo-Saxon Protestants like the Fairbankses were the predominant population group in the United States, especially in the lower Midwest, between the Civil War and World War I as the nation urbanized, industrialized, and expanded with twelve new states. A new middle class was developing and becoming dominant. Many became wealthy and comfortable. They were patriotic and concerned, to one degree or another, for one reason or another, about factory workers, rural citizens, and immigrants. The technology of the time—telegraph, telephone, railroads, and readily available daily newspapers—made nationwide communication and transportation convenient and accessible.[1] In the four decades between 1875 and 1915, everyday life was characterized by inequities between gilded wealth and dark poverty. While people of the time saw themselves as rugged individualists espousing traditional values, life was becoming more institutional and urban.[2] Charles Warren Fairbanks fit that pattern. He grew up on a farm and worked his way though college and law school, but he moved to a city and became an attorney for large corporations and a prominent member of the national Republican Party.

As Charles was establishing a law practice in Indianapolis, he and Nellie were starting a family. Their first child and only daughter, Adelaide, was born in 1875. Warren, Frederick, Richard, and Robert were born between 1878 and 1886. Their family life, kept private, was admired by close friends who saw the dignified lawyer and his charming wife become warm companions of their children in the seclusion of their home in the evenings.[3] Initially, it had been necessary for them to live modestly, at the very first in a boarding house. Nellie willingly economized. They made friends in Indianapolis. They joined Meridian Street Methodist Episcopal Church.[4] Early in marriage, Nellie studied law in order to help Charles prepare legal briefs, and he asked her to review manuscripts of his speeches, which were becoming more frequent.[5] He and his wife were "comrades"[6]—he found in her one who shared his struggles, his aspirations, and his successes.[7] In their home and social life, they were "not ostentatious, but always simple, kindly, and earnest."[8] Charles became a railroad attorney thanks to the help of his mother's two brothers: Charles Warren Smith, general manager of the Chesapeake and Ohio Railroad, and newspaperman William Henry Smith.[9] Charles represented a new type of lawyer. In contrast to an earlier generation of courtroom lawyers, he and many of his peers were corporate lawyers. He was able to specialize in reorganizing and investing in bankrupt railroads ultimately in South

America as well as in North America.[10] With skill and characteristic hard work—and help from Nellie—he rapidly began building a substantial fortune. As their circumstances became more affluent, they moved to increasingly commodious homes and were able to hire domestic servants. Because Nellie was a charming hostess, her entertaining was of great benefit to Charles's career. Their home in Indianapolis at the turn of the century was a frame house big enough for their family, "luxurious for its day, but simple and homelike and in excellent taste."[11] The beautiful, extensive garden delighted Mrs. Fairbanks, who personally oversaw the gardener's work. "Flowers are her pleasure, and the beds contain a large and varied collection."[12] She was also nurturing a varied collection of roles as a woman.

Charles Fairbanks's increasing investments included two thousand acres of rich farmland in central Illinois. The area was crossed by the Indianapolis, Bloomington, and Western Railroad, of which he was the attorney, and a branch of the Wabash Railroad, with which he had business dealings. He and one of his brothers, who lived and farmed in the area, established a railroad depot and grain elevator that became an active shipping point in the area. Another brother had a grain elevator in Chicago. Charles built a summer home in Blue Ridge Township, Piatt County, Illinois, on some of his rural property, easily accessible by train from Indianapolis. In order to be in touch with business and political interests, he had a long distance telephone installed in the home and telephones connecting the various parts of the family farms where cattle, grain, corn, and fine horses were raised.[13] Both Charles and Nellie enjoyed riding splendid horses.

In colloquialisms of the day, the *Indianapolis News* reported of the farm: "All the hands on the farm are carefully looked after. Among the colored hands a good brass band was organized. The men employed are watched and those who show an interest in their work are given an opportunity of taking a farm on shares where they have their own houses and are furnished teams and all farm implements."[14]

As the children were growing up in Indianapolis, the family and various ones of their relatives were able to spend time on the Illinois farm every summer. When Charles was in Indianapolis attending to business and politics, Nellie wrote from the farm[15] one July, "My Darling Charley, Your kind letters were received yesterday to my great pleasure. I hope nothing will happen to prevent your coming to see us and spend Sunday. It seems such a long time since the 4th which was the last time I saw my dear boy, a great deal more than two weeks. Yesterday Flo, Lulu, Freddie, and I went to Farmer City to do some shopping … Little Richard and Robert are playing on the boardwalk, and the patter of their bare feet can easily be heard in here, where I am writing. Fred is out in the 'big pasture' … and our farmer-boy Warren started before 4:30 for the Brown place where he is driving a rake. He is growing so brown and strong. We all want to see sister [Adelaide] so much but I dare say she is having a good time … Mother's [railroad] passes came yesterday and she will probably be in Indianapolis tonight as she is anxious to get there … I am, my darling boy, your loving Nellie."

Nellie Fairbanks was described by her friends as having distinguishing characteristics of "kindliness and a very gracious manner," never descending to unkind criticisms.[16] She was thoughtful, inspiring others by her life of earnestness, wisdom, and zeal. She had a fine mind, "the source of constant mental growth," strengthened by study, reading, and travel.[17] "She was a born leader, without malice or bitterness in her nature."[18] Contributing to her characteristics, her spiritual development continued from childhood throughout her life. As a devoted church member, her talents were "enhanced by her truly pious and lovely Christian character."[19]

In 1885, she established the first all-women's literary club in Indianapolis, the Fortnightly Literary Club, and was elected its first president. The motto was "Light seeking light doth light of light beguile," reminiscent of the motto of the Clionian Literary Society at Ohio Wesleyan Female College, "Light, More Light." According to its constitution, the object of the Fortnightly was to study literature, art, and social, political, and domestic science.[20]

There were several other active women's clubs in Indianapolis, including the Indianapolis Women's Club of which Mrs. Fairbanks was a member. In the 1880s, the Indianapolis Women's Club, under the leadership of educator and internationally known feminist May Wright Sewall, promoted the idea that local women's groups get together to exchange ideas. In 1888, Mrs. Sewall proposed that women organize a stock company with shares held only by women and transferable only to women. The purpose would be to construct, furnish, and maintain a building to be used for literary, artistic, scientific, industrial, musical, mechanical, and educational purposes for the public, particularly women. She had developed the idea after a speaking engagement in her native city, Milwaukee, the only other location in the country having an edifice built by women for similar activities. Cornelia Fairbanks was one of several hundred women who bought shares for twenty-five dollars each, one vote per share.[21] Mrs. Fairbanks was on the board of fifteen women that developed plans in 1888 and 1889 for this building, the Propylaeum, its name referring to the gathering place at the entrance of an ancient Greek temple. The Propylaeum would be a gateway to culture. Charles Fairbanks was one of four lawyers who helped carry out the legal requirements of the building project.[22] This unusual enterprise necessitated inquiry into several legal questions before the company could be organized. The laws of the time had to be stretched to allow women to be sole investors in, and operators of, a corporation. Experience planning a women's club building would serve Nellie well later.

The cornerstone was laid in 1890 and the building completed in 1891.[23] The group of women's clubs meeting at the Propylaeum was a predecessor of the national General Federation of Women's Clubs.[24] Women in many cities were discussing the feasibility of building such structures. Letters of inquiry came to Indianapolis from Massachusetts, Georgia, Minnesota, California, Michigan, Louisiana, and many other states.

An article by Bertha Damaris Knobe in *The Woman's Home Companion*, January 1899, described the Propylaeum as one of ten preeminent women's club facilities, elegant from "portico to pantry," that had been built in the ensuing decade along with an equal number of less pretentious women's club buildings. Prominent women from all over the country had come to celebrate the formal opening of the Romanesque Indianapolis structure, financed entirely by women. At Propylaeum gatherings, Cornelia Fairbanks had the opportunity to meet speakers and other guests from around the country and to develop acquaintances with women from many other states. Her political base was developing. The Fortnightly Literary Club was one of the first clubs to rent meeting space at the Propylaeum. Their program for 1892–1893 included a talk by Mrs. Fairbanks on national characteristics of the modern novel. The other topic of that day was local coloring of the modern novel, and the program noted, "A plea for the local in literature does not in the least imply disintegration of the national element in literature, and it is far removed from sectionalism." Other topics that year included the literatures of Germany, France, and the Scandinavian countries, contemporary art, Ignatius Loyola and the Jesuits, Moses Maimonides and charity, and the Americanization of new immigrants.[25]

The patriotic topic, education of new immigrants about American history and citizenship, addressed a cause that Nellie Fairbanks would continue to hold dear for the rest of her life. Mrs. Fairbanks was the first of two women elected in 1889 to the Indiana State Board of Charities, established as a reform of the supervision of prisons, mental hospitals, homes for soldiers and sailors and their orphans, and schools for the mentally retarded, deaf, and blind. Members of the board visited the institutions and compiled reports, making repeat visits to see whether suggested reforms had been instituted. She served until 1893.

The Board of Charities convened the first Indiana state conference on charities and correction in Indianapolis in 1890, and ultimately became a member of the National Conference of Charities and Correction. Recognition of urban poverty by Indiana reformers led to local settlement houses on the model of Jane Addams's Hull House in Chicago.[26] Nellie was developing a career in acceptable Victorian women's roles as Charles was building a career in business and politics. Family remained of paramount importance to both. In the spring of 1890, when Charles was in New York on business, Nellie wrote,[27] "My darling Charley, It already seems a long time since you went away, so much so that I am surprised there is nothing new to tell you, excepting that Mrs. Hess is to have a company on Friday and has asked me to receive with her, but I hardly think I can do so as I want to run over and see how Ma is getting on [in Marysville]. Warren and Richard went to spend their [spring] vacation in Illinois, started this morning, so that I shall not be able to go to Ohio until the [railroad] pass returns. I shall be gone just a few days, so as to send the pass to them to come home in time for school. Freddie as usual preferred to remain at home to going away anywhere. I am glad he is so fond of home. I did not finish my letter Monday so resume this Tuesday morning … I am thinking of spring bonnets this morning. It is a lovely morning, and Adelaide and I are going down to investigate the subject, so tremble as this may be high and dear in plural ways … This morning dawned beautifully, but just now shows how truly apropos the bard, when he said, 'the uncertain glory of an April day.' … Dr. Cleveland preached a beautiful sermon, Easter Sunday, but don't ask me for the text. I think I didn't hear it. The church was beautiful with lilies and palms; and all the pews were filled, people sitting in the aisle and the gallery filled. Willie wrote me [about the garden] seeds, I am going after them in a few minutes. Much love from all and more and most from me, Your Nellie."

She managed household affairs, sometimes requiring rapid replenishment of funds from Charles, and took care of the children in a day before immunizations and antibiotics.[28] "My darling Charley: Your more than kind answer to my telegram was just received. I am writing in the room with Freddie. He has been sick with a severe cold. I needed money to pay quite a number of grocery and dry goods accounts … wanted very much to get a picture for ourselves and I had subscribed to help buy one for the association … needed some funds. Thomas has been putting down the sod today … it will be about right I guess.— Wednesday a.m. Darling Charley, I didn't finish my letter yesterday so will do so this morning before the mail carrier arrives. Freddie is writing, too, and I am helping spell words so we may not get through in time after all—Yesterday at the club we had election of officers and had quite a spirited time voting … I have not been able to put out any plants yet at all and the children are begging me to sod over the horse shoe and have a tennis court on the ground. Mr. Combs, the florist, suggests that we take down the old apple tree and give that space, but I think this is such a picturesque feature. I dislike to part with it, so what would you do if you were here, and when are you coming home? – Shall I send regrets to Mr. and Mrs. J. E. Scott who wish us to play cards with them next Friday? I surely shall if you are not here as I am tired of going without you. We have just now received the cards of Gen. and Mrs. Carnahan, wanting us to be present evening of June 4 at their daughter's wedding reception.—I have not been well at all this week. I wish I might feel a lot better. Think I will take a tonic. Don't be alarmed, you know I am in the habit of thinking I have mortal illness when I feel a little under the weather. I am not really sick often enough to get used to it … Adelaide [age 15] is not doing what would wish her to. She has during the winter and at other times lost so much school that she has taken to weeping and studying her lessons at home and protesting she cannot pass her examinations. I wish you would write her a letter. I am going to see Miss Allen her teacher this afternoon. It seems as though she can not learn arithmetic, for that is her trouble. I think if she can not do better work, I will take her into public school and see if that will not take the conceit out of her. She imagines she can learn without study; but she is not of that class, if such a one exists, and it may excite her ambition if she is in a class with both boys and girls—Now I wish I had not bothered you when you are so busy, but I guess I will let it stand as I do not wish to write it over.—Warren and Richard are in school. Freddie would have gone this morning but he was threatened with pleurisy when he was sick Sunday and Monday, so I thought it best for him to stay out until entirely well." She inquired about their friends in New York, and signed, "Yours with love, Nellie."

Several months later, during a subsequent business trip by Charles to New York, Nellie wrote,[29] "My darling Charley, your most welcome and dear good letter came to hand last night about 5 o'clock on my return from Sunday School with our little flock, and we were all so glad that we stood up and read it, before we took off our wraps. Yesterday was a terrible rainy Sunday, but there was quite a large number of those who braved the dreary day and listened to a most magnificent discourse, one of the finest Dr. Cleveland has ever given us. It was founded upon the remarks of St. Paul that those who are strong must uphold those who are weak—and the subject was the beauty of unselfishness and discipline of different kinds of selfishness and their effects upon the character—it was a masterly … discourse.—I have Frederick out of school for a week, and so I thought while I did would take him over to Marysville for two or three days. Dr. Dunlap said it would be better for him while he took the medicine not to breathe so many different breaths in the crowded school rooms … his appetite is so much better, and he begins to look like our rosy round Fred boy again … Now don't be alarmed about this, for if you should see him you'd feel no alarm whatever. He is so well, and he is trying to be careful, keeps on his coat if he is warm from running and playing, and you know that is something unusual for Frederick!" She noted invitations they had received and suggested entertaining several friends at dinner on his return; she sent regards to friends in New York. Then she mentioned the election of a U.S. Senator by the Indiana Legislature, as was done at the time. Some of their friends said "that there was no doubt who would have had it because the people were much dissatisfied with the management … Of course, it does not amount to very much but there it shows something of the feeling for my candidate." Two others both said "that they would have Mr. Fairbanks for senator—next time anyway." She mentioned social activities, including an invitation for Adelaide to be a bridesmaid. "I sent you an *Indianapolis News* containing an item about you and your first speech … Did you receive it? I received the *Mail and Express* and read your interview. Miss Laura read it. She said that was a correct statement of affairs all but the part of the Republicans rallying in '92— she thinks the Democrats, but she is always a little bit tinctured with Democratic bias.—Robert has just been here kissing me for Papa. I will close again. Yours, Nellie." A brief scrawled note to "Papa" from four-year-old Robert followed her signature. The Democrats won elections in Indiana in 1890.[30] Democrat Grover Cleveland won the presidential election in 1892, and Democrats again won Indiana state offices.[31] Charles Fairbanks's time in national politics had not yet arrived. While Nellie was a wife and mother in Indianapolis, she made frequent visits to her family in Ohio. Her father, Judge Philander B. Cole, continued to practice law in Marysville until his death of heart failure in 1892, at age seventy-six. Nellie traveled from Indianapolis to be with him in his final days.[32]

When caring for her children in Indianapolis, she feared childhood illnesses, which were frequently serious or even fatal at the time, especially diphtheria. She used the remedies of the day, including ointments and syrups.[33] "My darling Charley: You have been gone four days and have not written me yet, but for all that I am secretly writing you. The children are all well and I am engaged each evening in greasing and dosing them to keep them so ... I have been not so very well, but nearly all the time I have been taking good care although I did go down stairs to see about the sitting rooms, but the house was nice and warm, and I think I did not take cold. Mr. and Mrs. Van Camp had to recall their invitations in honor of Mrs. Harrison and Mrs. McKee because of scarlatina ["scarlet fever," streptococcal rash and fever] in their family.— Dollie [her sister] and I are going to Rushville tomorrow [to see brother Ulysses and his family] to remain until Saturday. I shall take Frederick with me as I know he will ... take cold if I do not watch over him. He is getting nice and stout I think.— Mr. C. E. Coffin wants you to attend a dinner party next week he will give in honor of the Stewards and Ministers of the church.—Nancy Baker wrote you a note thanking you for what you did in getting her the position, saying she was the happiest girl in the world because she had this way of helping herself.—The children are all in school this morning excepting Frederick. He is not because Dr. Dunlap wrote me that, while there was nothing suspicious looking about his throat, yet while the disease was so prevalent he would not put him in school. No one in this neighborhood has diphtheria at all so far as I can hear, but many people are taking their children out of school through fear. Hoping to hear from you soon dear Charley, with love and kisses from us all, Your loving Nellie."

In the midst of it all, she missed Charley very much. "Monday Evening, January 26, 1891, My darling Charley, This time o'night is much later than I would be sitting up if you were here, and that I know; nevertheless I will write a few lines to you.—The Board of State Charities met today and the Governor wants the board to 'tackle' the books of Warden Murdock of the Prison. The board seems disinclined to do so. But Gov. is in dead earnest about it I think. It hardly seems as though it can since the legislature have a committee for the purpose of investigating the Warden. I expect [another board member] wishes he would not be so notice taking of it as to draw attention to another law neglected." She added news of friends: a photo of a new baby, someone's twins with colic. "I don't know of anything to tell you except I would love much to see you and that the children are all well and apparently happy. Likewise the same may be said of their grandparents." She asked that he go to a certain wedding in New York if he could, noting that she had sent a gift, purchased with a check "which must have made a large rift in my account" and concluded, "With kindest, dear Charley, your own Nellie."

At times, in addition to news of, and concerns about, the children, Nellie expressed concerns about her own health. Three years after the above letter, she wrote,[34] "My Dearest Charley, Your poking fun letter came just now. I had to smile much at it for it sounded like life, so natural was it, story and all … I will say the little boys are well and romping to their hearts content in the leisure of their enforced vacation. They and their crowd went skating this afternoon, but did not stay long. It grew so cold so rapidly. It is now six degrees and they have gone up to bed. Little darlings. Robert went to sleep in the dining room, and Richard led him up stairs, and I came in the library to write the Papa dear my daily chat.—This morning I arose rather late and felt fine … but alack and alas … grippy ["la grippe," influenza] symptoms set in … I had that little growth which has been making so much trouble removed, and I felt quite nervous and achy all this afternoon; and after I finish writing to my good boy, I will join the remnant of the home back upstairs and woo balm sleep." She mentioned a letter from Adelaide at Ohio Wesleyan University, the first she had written in the new semester, and that lodging with a professor there had been arranged for Warren. "I am so glad of it. I shall feel better about him now. I suppose he is too busy to write … We must drop in and see them soon when the weather is better than now. They would like it so much.—I think my ears and various other parts of my anatomy have obtruded themselves upon my attention, notwithstanding I am a great deal better today than yesterday. I am glad to know you are making arrangements to hasten your homeward return. I will expect to see you Sunday at all events. I have informed everyone that you will probably be home at the end of this week although you have not said so … as to my telephoning '40 times' per diem that is 'a error' … and once in awhile two days pass without exchanging of visits. Now what do you think of that?" She mentioned news from the relatives on the farm in Illinois and that illness there had not been as serious as they had thought. "Such is my hope at any rate … The passes came this morning for me to go to N.Y. How I wish it were so I could go. I should enjoy being there with you so much if I were only well enough to go, but I know I am not. I shall certainly not worry, so you kindly say. For me not to, anymore than it is my 'worrisome nature' will order. I know not why it is, but I am constantly bothering myself about something or one or all of absent somebodies who are dearer to me than the ruddy drops that visit my heart, namely the Papa dear and his three largest children and the two dear little ones likewise, especially if they are out of my sight. How perturbed a thing is the heart of a woman, where it sees not its loved ones near. Hoping soon to see my dearest boy. I will say a final good night and hie me to my little bed. With tenderest love, Your Nellie."

The next day she replied to a letter received after hers was mailed.[35] "My dearest Charley, Your nice long letter came this evening. I love much to get them. They mark a happy spot for me in each day … The reason you have divined truly, I did not feel able to write the first week of your absence. I was not very sick, excepting so languid, and powerful aching. I did not feel inclined to hold up my head. And consequently my letter writing powers were drooping, but I am so much better now. I think I shall be greatly better since the removal of the obstruction yesterday.—I went down the street this morning and sent Adelaide the hat she requested, paid a few bills, and hastened home. Took my lunch alone as Robert and Richard were through theirs … Richard and some other little boys were going skating on a pond … and they were in a hurry to start out. The nipping air made them equally in haste to return, as oft times, as they came back very cold. Robert and Bert Coffin made a bonfire on the common in order to procure charcoal with which to black themselves. As a result, the boys are both very sleepy and in bed quite a long time … The other evening I let the little boys have a little party which May attended to for them. I was not worried a bit with it, and it made them so happy. You know they felt lonely without the other boys and this seemed to cheer them greatly … I didn't tell you Papa dear because I feared you would not only think I had been worrying with it; but thought since the dear good Papa wants to know all that happens he must know that too. They got it up to celebrate another day out of school. Ardent students are they not? ... Yes, dear, I am anxious about the little boys. There seems to be so much trouble about diphtheria in this part of town. Of course, we must not say anything about it, but I would be glad on that account to be where there is better sewerage. But this place is endeared to me by so many things. It is our first own home here. The children played, sung, and swung in the old apple tree here. Adelaide and Warren planted their little peach trees. Here grows Adelaide's crab apple tree, Warren's apple trees, Freddie's and Richard's maples. Almost every plant and bush has something to make it dear to us. For you and I have watched children, plants ... all grow in this ground. How many times we have strolled around and taken in the cool evening and freeing morning air. It is really a nice place, isn't it dear? Well, I will close now as Charles is going out and will carry this to the P.O. for me.—Dr. Spinkie [Dr. Mary Spink] dropped in, 'happened in,' to dinner and stayed till a quarter of seven. She had to hasten away as she has some more curious cases placed under her care in the last day or two. We were reading some French history in the little library. She said, 'How lovely it is here. I wish I could stay, but I must away to work.' I think she is better now than she has been for several days. She looked worn and bilious [sickly], but she said it was 'La Grippe' working upon her.—I wrote Frederick today and have not had a letter yet. Write soon dearest boy, Your Nellie."

Nurturing her children and participating in community activities, Nellie Fairbanks ultimately chose, characteristically, to join a patriotic organization. In 1895, she became a member of the Carolyn Scott Harrison Chapter of the Daughters of the American Revolution (DAR), named for the first national DAR president, wife of United

Chapter Five

DESTINED TO BE A LEADER

Meanwhile, Charles Fairbanks was rising to prominence as a politician. Indiana historian James H. Madison observed that the 1890s showed him at his shrewdest. "He knew that the basis for political advancement rested largely on support from dozens of local and county politicians, the men who helped elect state legislators, who in turn [at that time] elected United States Senators. Using his time and money, Fairbanks developed a network of political correspondents and friends throughout Indiana."[1] He wrote letters of encouragement to local politicians, asked their advice, congratulated them on their election victories, and provided them with free railroad passes.[2] He bought part interest in the *Indianapolis News* with his uncle William Henry Smith and later the *Indianapolis Journal,* adding to opportunities for enhancing his political efforts. His silent partnership in the *News,* while running for public office, was seen as scandalous by progressive opponents when it was revealed later. The *News,* although supporting his candidacies, did not necessarily agree with his views in its editorials. Because of close family ties, Charles Fairbanks assented to the wishes of its independent young editor, his cousin Delavan Smith.[3]

Nellie was a gracious hostess to any political acquaintances of Charles who visited, greeting them personally and making them feel at home. Chances are she discussed politics—discreetly, of course. She also managed home and family during her husband's political travels around the state and to speaking engagements elsewhere.

In his rise to national politics, Charles Fairbanks developed a friendship with fellow Ohioan and Methodist William McKinley, nine years his senior. Fairbanks was a member of the inner circle of Ohio politician Mark Hanna, who successfully promoted McKinley's nomination at the 1896 Republican National Convention in St. Louis. As temporary chairman of the convention, Fairbanks gave the keynote speech. According to the *St. Louis Globe Democrat*, "His appearance was in his favor, and he spoke deliberately and plainly, but he labored under the disadvantage of being obliged to read from a manuscript which puts the best oratorical efforts out of the question. The unusual length of the address was another drawback, and, in spite of its literary merit, it grew tiresome after a time."[4] No doubt, Charles and Nellie made note of reactions to his speech for future reference. Fairbanks hadn't made a big hit as an orator, but he had received national recognition and was on his way to the national capital. He was elected to the Senate from Indiana that year having worked to swing Indiana votes to McKinley, who became president of the United States.[5]

Nellie Fairbanks, in many ways representative of the "true womanhood" of the nineteenth century, was a handsome woman with reddish brown hair and brown eyes, attentive to her husband and five children. She became active in women's clubs considered appropriate for the gentle sex. But she understood law and politics, shared the struggles of each with her husband, and was rapidly gaining parliamentary and administrative experience. She had learned about state politics first hand during her service on the Indiana Board of Charities. After Charles was elected to the United States Senate from Indiana, in November 1896, they moved to Washington, D.C., with their family. They would be there for the winter seasons and return to Indianapolis in the summers. The True Woman of the nineteenth century was becoming the New Woman of the twentieth. She was entering the national political arena as the wife of a senator and would hold elective office herself in national women's organizations. This "gracious, intensely vital woman"[6] was coming into her own. Historian Margaret Gibbons Wilson described the transition in women's roles as a time when the New Woman was alternately praised or damned by contemporary commentators. In contrast to women of the past, her supporters saw her as "more independent, better educated, a companion to husband and children," and "not ashamed to know something of the administration of the city, state, or Nation." She saw herself as "part of a group working to make the world more beautiful for all." Her detractors perceived her to be "younger than she looked, dark ('for fairness usually goes with an interest in children, and other gentle weaknesses'), very intelligent, not pretty, with an 'aggressive air of independence.' Moreover, she was unhappy. She failed in her attempt 'to prove that woman's mission is something higher than the bearing of children and bringing them up.'"[7] Nellie Fairbanks was described as a complex woman—devoted to family and home, but not to domesticity; feminine, but a suffragist and proponent of the rights of women.[8] By all accounts, she was happy. She was intelligent, mature, and a handsome woman with brown hair and eyes, neither dark nor fair, and very much interested in her children. A woman journalist described her fashion sense: "Always dressed in perfect taste, Mrs. Fairbanks renders her gowns in keeping with her position rather than as a matter of superlative importance. New modes and latest fashion wrinkles trouble her not at all, nor will she consent to being made uncomfortable by modes that hamper. Certain limitations of national politics, the personal story of railroad lawyer Fairbanks was more complicated than his progressive critics made out. Sticking to the party line of conservative Republicans while earning the respect of other senators, Fairbanks performed competently in his eight years in the Senate. He conducted no private law practice during those years. As chairman of the Immigration Committee, he favored immigration restrictions and required literacy tests.[14] He chaired the Committee on Public Buildings and Grounds, an appointment that would become instructive and helpful to Nellie.

McKinley appointed Fairbanks chairman of the American delegation to the Joint-High Commission with Britain to settle the boundary dispute between Canada and Alaska in 1898 and 1899. Fairbanks declared, to popular approval, "I am opposed to the yielding of an inch of United States territory."[15] A settlement of the boundary was not reached at that time. Fairbanks had no diplomatic experience and was concerned about his political future as a potential presidential candidate. Concessions to the British would alienate Irish and German voters at home. Moreover, his task was almost impossible in that he would need to negotiate a settlement that would be ratified by a two-thirds majority of his fellow senators. The dispute was finally settled by other officials in 1903 after deadlocked meetings in Washington and London.[16] The people of Alaska did appreciate his hard work on their behalf. They named a city for him, Fairbanks, his most well-known legacy today.

Back home in Indiana, he was dealing with Senator Albert Beveridge, who was cast much more in the mold of Theodore Roosevelt than that of Charles Fairbanks. He was charismatic, a dramatic orator, and a proponent of the new manifest destiny, "control of the world's trade and acquisition of great colonies."[17] Progressive politicians were often imperialists. While Beveridge was promoting his views throughout

Indiana, Senator Fairbanks was busy working on settlement of the Canada-Alaska border. In 1899 the Indiana General Assembly elected Beveridge to the Senate—a "surprising event that marked a turning point in Indiana politics."[18] Young reformers supporting Beveridge were now pitted against the old guard of the state's Republican Party under the leadership of Fairbanks. McKinley's assassination and Roosevelt's resulting presidency tipped the balance of power between Indiana's senators. Beveridge was closer to Roosevelt not only temperamentally but also politically. Fairbanks was re-elected to the United States Senate for his second term in 1903. In his acceptance speech to the state legislature, he said, "We are not to be led by the consciousness of increased national power and prestige to be come an international meddler. We are not to put upon the high seas fleets to disturb the peace of the world"—in direct contradiction to Beveridge's imperialist position.[19] He supported international peace efforts until the United States entered World War I fourteen years later.

Both Indiana senators were mentioned as possible running mates for Roosevelt in 1904. However, Beveridge was more interested in another term in the United States Senate. They compromised: Beveridge would not hinder Fairbanks's bid for the vice presidential nomination; Fairbanks would not stand in the way of Beveridge's second term in the United States Senate. The arrangement worked. Beveridge stayed in the senate; Fairbanks became vice president.[42] Ultimately, this worked better for Fairbanks who, as presiding officer, was able to block some legislation that Beveridge favored and Fairbanks did not.[20]

During this time, Mrs. Fairbanks was becoming nationally prominent in her own right. When Charles began his first term in the Senate of the United States, she was a delegate to the Continental Congress of the Daughters of the American Revolution that met in an auditorium not far from the Capitol where the U.S. Senate met. Mrs.

Adlai E. Stevenson, of Illinois, a former president of the DAR and wife of Grover Cleveland's vice president, wrote, "I recall distinctly Mrs. Fairbanks's first appearance upon the floor of the Continental Congress in 1898. It was soon apparent that she had parliamentary usage at her command, was familiar with the subjects under discussion, and kept well in hand the proceedings upon the floor. She sat at the head of her [Indiana] delegation, immediately in front of the platform, and her 'Madam President General' was pronounced in such a forceful, yet pleasing manner as to attract my fixed attention. I saw at once that she was destined to be a leader. She had a quick grasp of conditions, spoke with ease and elegance, and had the gift of repartee which gave a personal touch to her remarks." [21]

The public lives of Senator and Mrs. Fairbanks intertwined in many ways. Senator Fairbanks opposed the Spanish-American war at first, as did McKinley, but supported President McKinley when war was declared.[22] Mrs. Fairbanks participated in efforts to help soldiers. The Daughters were concerned about the fact that families of the men who had gone to the front were in need and the soldiers and sailors were lacking many comforts. A War Committee was formed to raise a fund to help military men and their families. Mrs. Fairbanks was appointed to a subcommittee that had charge of disbursements of the fund.[23] In their private life as well, the war came close to the Fairbanks's home. Their eldest son, Warren Charles Fairbanks, was a captain in an Indiana regiment during the war.

Senator Fairbanks had incredible self-control, speaking only after deliberate reflection and with caution to avoid any commitment for fear of losing support from those who disagreed. "But his speeches were always kept on a high moral plane, devoid of demagoguery, vituperation, irony, or sarcasm. Never did he deal in personalities or abuse his opponents."[24] One controversial stand of Fairbanks in the

Senate was to agree with African-American Indiana soldiers in the war with Spain that they have African-American, not white, officers. Unlike any other state at the time, Indiana adopted this policy for its militia units.[25] Fairbanks's neighbors in Ohio when he was a young man provided a station on the Underground Railroad, and his father took the part of his African-American farm hands when white farm hands showed prejudice.[26]

He looked like a president of the United States—tall and dignified in his Prince Albert coat—but he never became one. He was considered a potential presidential or vice presidential candidate in the first two decades of the twentieth century and was promoted by friends. At the urging of advisors, McKinley chose as his running mate in 1900—not his friend Fairbanks, another conservative Midwesterner—but, rather, the popular, ebullient, progressive New Yorker Theodore Roosevelt.

Fairbanks, the skilled behind-the-scenes politician, quite capable of compromise when necessary, said in his final speech to the Senate when leaving the vice presidency in 1909, "The Senate of the United States was designed by our fathers to be a deliberative chamber in the fullest and best sense—a chamber where the passions of the hour might be arrested and where the better judgment of the people would find ultimate expression."[27]

When he left Washington after eight years in the Senate plus four years as its presiding officer, the *Washington Post* reported that he had been "a valuable public servant, an able, dignified, and kind man, and a splendid host." He came as "one of the best lawyers in the middle west" and was seen to grow "to prominence as one of the leaders of the Senate" over which he presided as vice president "with exceptional dignity."[28]

It was said of Mrs. Fairbanks, "Those who know Mrs. Fairbanks [in Indianapolis] have long been aware of the influence that she exercises with the senator in political matters. He respects her judgment and defers to it. All of his public speeches are submitted to her criticism, and her advice is asked on important points. Nor do the criticisms fall heedlessly. Manuscripts are revised if Mrs. Fairbanks so advises."[29] The same woman journalist continued, "The senator makes it a practice to read his speeches to his wife in the quiet of the home library, and if passed upon favorably, they are delivered to the larger audiences in the Senate or on the political platform. Mrs. Fairbanks will assist in planning her husband's campaign work [for vice president in 1904] in an advisory way." She wrote further that close friends had believed Mrs. Fairbanks to have played a part in influencing her husband to accept the nomination to run with Roosevelt. "Perhaps she is the more ambitious for honor and power."[30]Another view, suggesting that Mrs. Fairbanks was by no means naïve about politics, was that the "charge has been made against Mrs. Fairbanks that her ambition for social rank induced Senator Fairbanks to accept the nomination for Vice President. Her intimates [in Washington] laugh at this assertion, for nothing could be farther from the truth. On the contrary, she was averse to the proposition. Mrs. Fairbanks is not a woman to be content with second honors. Doubtless she believes, with good reason, that nonparticipation in this campaign [for vice president with Roosevelt] would have insured a higher attainment in the next [as Roosevelt's successor]."[31] Obviously, this complex woman's private views were difficult to categorize. But no one seems to have thought that she was uninterested in politics or naïve about furthering her husband's political career—or her own, for that matter.

Whatever her ambitions, Mrs. Fairbanks did most successfully enjoy the social life which enhanced her husband's standing in the nation's capital. Increasing personal freedom as her children grew older and the social status of a senator's wife in official Washington opened opportunities for her talents, and her husband's wealth made it possible to entertain frequently and well. She became a member of prestigious Washington women's clubs. She was a social leader, "her brilliant seasons in Washington having established her reputation as one of the most popular, graceful and tactful hostesses of the official set."[32] "Few women could have risen to prominence so rapidly and have borne themselves with such perfect poise. [A prominent Washington society woman was reported to have said,] 'She is the only woman in official life who enters a drawing room without self-consciousness and without seeking to associate herself immediately with persons of great influence.'" She was no respecter of persons.[33]

During their stay in Washington, Charles and Nellie Fairbanks saw their children complete college. The eldest, their daughter Adelaide, and eldest son Warren graduated from their parents' alma mater, Ohio Wesleyan University, to which the Fairbanks retained close ties. Charles was a member of the Board of Trustees for many years, and Nellie was elected an honorary member of the Phi Beta Kappa chapter.[34] At first, the younger boys were enrolled in preparatory schools in the East nearer their parents' new home and later entered college. Their son Frederick was a Princeton graduate, while Richard and Robert were Yale men.[35]

Just after graduation from college, Adelaide became engaged to a young surgeon, Dr. Horace Allen, who was twenty-five. He was a graduate of Yale and a medical college in New York City and had taken over his father's practice in Indianapolis. But Senator Fairbanks would not give permission for her to marry him. Charles and Nelllie returned to Indianapolis during the summer recess of Congress in August 1897 and announced to Adelaide that they had planned an extended trip in the East for her. Adelaide and the young doctor assumed that this meant that her parents were trying to separate them. Dr. Allen quickly and quietly got a friend to obtain a license and a minister, and he and Adelaide were married the next day at the friend's home with two couples at witnesses.[36] The senator's objections to the marriage were prophetic. The couple was divorced five years later, in December 1902. Adelaide claimed cruelty, neglect, and failure to contribute to her support. The surgeon was represented in court by his lawyer. Adelaide obtained restoration of her maiden name and the costs of her attorney's fees.[37] She moved to Washington to live with her parents. New romance awaited her there.

Although Senator and Mrs. Fairbanks had denied that Adelaide would soon be married, announcements were sent out in early September 1903 that Adelaide would be married on September 19 to Ensign John W. Timmons, USN, a graduate of the Naval Academy. They had met some years before while students at Ohio Wesleyan University. He was from a respectable, but not wealthy, Ohio family. She was not yet the daughter of a nationally prominent politician. Their college romance ended when he was appointed to Annapolis and moved east to a life of busy study and duties, and she returned to Indianapolis.

Years later, the two met again in Cleveland at the home of Ohio Senator Mark Hanna whom Charles Fairbanks had assisted in obtaining the nomination and election of McKinley in 1896. The college relationship was renewed. Ensign Timmons proposed; Adelaide was uncertain; then he received orders for a tour of duty overseas. In a note to her, he included a quotation from Indiana poet James Whitcomb Riley. It was her favorite line from a favorite poet whom she knew personally: "When care has cast her anchor in the harbor of a dream."[38] She accepted his proposal of marriage before his ship sailed. When he returned, they were married at her parents' Washington home in a quiet ceremony for family and close friends. Adelaide was described as "one of the distinctly beautiful young society women of Washington."[39] Ironically, some of Ensign Timmons's relatives in Ohio were concerned

Chapter Six

FRONTIERS

Nellie Fairbanks loved to travel, and her husband's position gave her opportunity to do so. While he was chairing the Joint High Commission to settle the Canada-Alaska border, Senator and Mrs. Fairbanks and their youngest son, Robert, traveled to Alaska in the summer of 1899. The territory had been purchased from Russia in 1867. Gold had been discovered in 1896, and the Klondike gold rush ensued in the Yukon area of Canada and Alaska. Sixty years after the Fairbankses visited, in 1959, the territory of Alaska became the forty-ninth state of the United States.

She kept notes on her travels and used them to prepare talks presented to various clubs and organizations to which she belonged. She spoke to the Washington Literary Club about the Alaska trip.[1]

"It was my good fortune to be a member of a party which, on June 14, sailed from Seattle for a cruise in Alaskan waters upon the graceful, staunch and swift McCulloch, known to fame as 'Dewey's dispatch boat' [in the Spanish-American War]. It was not in the dull gray paint given vessels in war time, but in pure white, emblematic of its peaceful errand, its home pennant floating gaily in the breeze as it steamed out of the harbor.

"I wish I might describe this trip from Skagway and return (for our voyage was so arranged that we did not revisit any place) so that you might also see the beauties of sea, mountain and sky, the shimmering waterfalls, glittering glaciers, roaring mountain torrents, and the golden roseate hues of the Alaskan sunset. These and many other things of interest I may not hope to describe adequately, but I shall be happy if I may be so fortunate as to convey a suggestion of what I saw and heard.

"Reference to the hasty notes taken of the trip unfolds to me a panoramic view of the entire scene. First, Departure Bay, where we spent a day or two coaling, anchored among its picturesque islets; then the Gulf of Georgia, with a homelike name but a most foreign appearance. I notice Queen Charlotte Sound, where, disturbed by a little rolling from the open sea, I fell an ignominious victim to 'mal de mer.' Prince of Wales Island is so bleak and forbidding that it seems unjust that the sunny, affable scion of royalty who now bears this title should share it with this inhospitable islet of a northern sea. We passed through Behm Canal, which our British cousins think should be the boundary between British Columbia and Alaska, but the land we passed did not receive favorable mention in the notebook, as it remarks: 'It seems worth little trouble unless its sterile, rocky surface is filled with gold.' Wrangell Narrows bring to mind the interesting but tortuous passage through a network of islands, sometimes low and crowded with verdure, sometimes rising into lofty, rocky banks on either side, so that it seemed we were creeping through a walled passage. After leaving the barren shore of British Columbia it was a perfect delight on approaching Baranof Island and entering the harbor of Sitka to have our eyes refreshed by a glimpse of the pretty modern home of the Governor, with its trim, thrifty, carefully attended garden, growing vegetables and flowers.

"Sitka is a quaint looking village more than a hundred years old, with a picturesque mixture of old Russian log houses, some new rough frame houses occupied by the natives, a few modern cottages, a large building used for a Russian orphanage mission school of the Presbyterian Home Missionary society, Sheldon Jackson Museum of Implements made and used by natives for hunting, fishing, and domestic use, their boats, sledges, and similar articles. To the careful observer it is like a pictorial history of the people and their manners and customs.

"The most conspicuous object in the town as one enters the harbor is the Russian church, a large frame building surmounted by an Oriental looking dome. This church is a most interesting one, containing valuable paintings presented by various Russian families as tokens of their admiration and appreciation of those who left their homes to found this church in Alaska. These pictures are framed in gold, pressed down in such a manner that it appears a part of the painting rather than the frame. There are various altars standing in the audience room of the church; each of them is called a church. Directly in the center there is placed a separate pulpit for the Bishop when he officiates. At the rear of the room is a stationary pulpit, directly in the rear of this a door opens into the Holy of Holies. But the profaning foot of woman is never suffered within the sanctuary, although the Russian professor, Pepoff, who escorted us through the church, clothed the prohibition in the kindly phrase 'only men members of the Greek Church are allowed to enter.' The people stand during worship, no seats being used by either priests or people.

"The old Russian fur warehouse is a relic of the old regime, as is a building now used for an American reading room. Both of these buildings are old, and the last is tottering to dissolution. The natives dwell close to the water's edge along the bay, no longer in their separate lodges or 'tepees,' but in the large frame houses, nearly air tight and heated by stoves. The result of this change of living is that the Indians, or natives, are no longer so strong or active as when they had plenty of fresh air and exercise, but they are listless often and weak-eyed, not at all like the 'noble red man' of song and story. There is no doubt that the natives are of Japanese origin, for they have all the characteristics of that race except that they are taller and of a stronger build. The natives are not particularly good looking but have not the saturnine and sullen expression which so many Indians of the plains have. They have a fine scorn of being called Indians, saying 'we are natives.'

"As soon as a vessel enters the harbor the entire native population immediately seize their household gods and goods and, rushing wildly, range themselves along the one board walk in the place, which extends from the dock through the town, holding up their various articles to tempt the roving fancy of the passing tourist. The Alaskan baskets are famous and are always paraded. They take their horn spoons out of their dinner pots and sell them; they take their silver bracelets from their arms. Copies of the totems, bead shoes, anything and everything is for sale for Sitkin dollar (50 cents) and upwards.

"These ingenious children of nature have a disconcerting manner of breaking into a loud, shrill laughter at the expense of anyone who lucklessly prices, vainly tries to cheapen, and then does not buy their goods.

"We leave quaint Sitka, with pleasant recollections of the affable, kindly officials and people and the courteous Governor and Mrs. Brady, all of whom made us welcome and our stay enjoyable. When next we see this somewhat insufficient capital of so vast a territory there will be many changes, doubtless, as the Department of Agriculture will have its experiment station on the site of Baronof Castle, the first Russian gubernatorial residence, and there will be, in addition to the 300 different kinds of wild flowers, which now flourish in Sitka, all the varieties of flowers and vegetables which grow in temperate climates. In place of the one-ox team and cart of the Agricultural department and the one-horse and two-seated wagon of the mission school, there may be many vehicles for work and pleasure. Possibly by that time (if far enough in the future) a little more attention will be given to the inhabitants of Alaska, so they may have unquestioned right to their own property that capital and enterprise may securely and advantageously be invested there.

"Muir Glacier came next to Sitka in the note book. It was a bright, beautiful day, June 23 when we entered Glacier Bay, and the vigilant Captain Francis, the most unerring of Alaskan pilots, steered our ship through ice floes and past many icebergs, glistening like crystals with vivid blue tints shining through the frozen snow until we were within 1,500 feet of the greatest of glaciers. I experienced a feeling of awe, and I think everyone was quieted before this wonderful demonstration of nature. It is a mile and a half across its front and 251 feet in height. It is solid ice fluted and corrugated with various shapes, like faces, spires, building, and animals. It grows in sublimity as one gazes. A hundred Niagara's, frozen and united would, perhaps, equal in grandeur Muir Glacier, that vast river of ice ever slowly and imperceptibly moving to the sea.

"Juneau is the next important point. It is a thriving city of perhaps 5,000 inhabitants, and although it has nothing but frame buildings closely crowded together, owing to the limited space on which it stands, yet it has of the modern improvements electric light, telephone, water works, as well as schools, churches, and theaters. It is claimed that its business establishments transact business amounting to millions of dollars every year. It stands at the foot of Mount Juneau, which is 3,000 or 4,000 feet in height. There is no doubt Juneau is the commercial metropolis of southeastern Alaska. There is the native village here of

Klington Indians whose chief Johnson, called upon us on the McCulloch and kindly invited us to see a dance performed by one of his tribe, arrayed in a beautiful ceremonial blanket, wearing a hideous mask, and decorated with feathers. The chief himself was dressed in a striking costume of cardinal velvet, elaborately embroidered, and he remained in dignified pose upon the stairway while his follower disported himself in most strange and fantastic manner in the dance. Mrs. Johnson is a woman of attractive appearance with a mild, intelligent expression. She is of the Bear family, while the chief is a member of another tribe, it not being allowable for members of the same tribe or family to intermarry. This woman on dress occasions mars her appearance by wearing a ring in the nose.

"Our next point of interest was Skagway, a thriving town of 3,000, situated in a wind swept cañon on the tempestuous water the Lynn Canal. Here where a little more than two years ago stood a dense forest of firs, hemlock, and pine there is today an active, energetic people, who have cleared the forest, built houses, laid out street and avenues, have a magnificent system of docks, a railroad leading over the mountains up to the summit through the White Pass to the Yukon region. They have law and order, to pay deference and obedience; all this done by themselves, as they have no law making them an incorporated town, but their teachings and instructions range them on the right side. It was amusing to read on the side of a plain, not over large structure 'Fifth Avenue Hotel,' and it sounded strange indeed in this town, where the stumps are just being moved, to hear a woman say, 'My number is 25 Broadway.' I was struck with the bravery and hopefulness of both men and women, in their happy, energetic ways, though I doubt not they have moments of depression in their pioneer lives, even though they are full of activity and fascination. Whatever I inferred I heard no murmur. The hospitality and whole-heartedness with which they made us welcome to their town and homes were genuine and beautiful.

"One afternoon they gave us a musical entertainment. Another day we were entertained in a large house built of logs and covered with a large canvass roof. Here the women brought all their household treasures, fur rugs, baskets, pictures, and a piano, and here the whole town came to take us by the hand and inquire about the States, as well as the boundary question, in which they were vitally interested. Some people were in full evening dress, others in any plain costume they had. Some of the frozen, hardy miners came just as they arrived from the mines in sweaters and high boots, little boys and girls, large ones, too, businessmen, natives, everybody, old and young, heartily greeting us. One noticeable feature of the reception was the absence of old people. There are few besides young and middle aged there.

"We were taken to the summit of the White Pass by the courtesy of the railroad company, and a most wonderful ride it was, and more marvelous in the wonderful feat of engineering which was accomplished when the road was built over heights and wide, deep cañons. It is this road, giving the direct and comparatively easy route to the Yukon [gold mines] which will save Skagway from the fate of its once rival 'Dead Eyes.' It is needless to say that much of interest must remain untold, even in so long a paper, and so I may not take you to Haines Mission, Pyramid Harbor, Kasaan, nor to the magnificent scenery of Rudyard Cove, called the Yosemite of Alaska.

"Alaska is true to its name, which signifies 'the great country,' great in every phase of the work with its placid, island-dotted inland sea, its forbidding yet alluring mountains seamed with yellow gold, its rivers and lakes, thronged with finny multitude which furnishes occupation and food for another multitude, its 20,000 miles of coast, its native population offering a field for the true missionary and philanthropist.

The existence of the Russian Greek Church affords subject for reflection for the Christian and the American.

"No one can see Alaska and fail to be impressed with the fact that it is a great neglected territory. The Governor has merely a semblance of authority; they have no Delegate in Congress to look after their interests and rights; the citizens have no right to lands for horticultural or agricultural purposes. The children of Americans have inadequate schooling. These complaints of Alaskan people merit redress."

Charles and Nellie Fairbanks had heard many tales of another frontier as they were growing up, only a couple of generations removed from pioneers in Ohio. Charles's ancestors came from Wales to New England in the 1600s, and one of them from Vermont later served in the Revolutionary War. His son, Charles's grandfather, moved to Union County, Ohio, in the early 1800s.[2] Nellie's maternal great-grandfather, Elijah Witter, lived on the frontier in Pennsylvania in the midst of battles between settlers and Native Americans. His house was burned three times. He was chosen by neighbors to look after the women and children as they stayed in their cabins during the fighting. They were often short of provisions, once necessitating a daring journey by Nellie's great-grandmother who rode fifty miles on horseback to obtain salt and returned safely in spite of encountering a number of Native Americans. Nellie's grandfather, David Witter, had been a trapper, hunter, and farmer, and a soldier in the New York militia in the War of 1812. He and his first wife, her grandmother, moved to Ohio as some of the first settlers in 1814 or 1815. He raised cattle, marketing his herds in Philadelphia and Detroit. He was also in the real estate business and in 1828 built a brick hotel in Marysville. One of the best known men in Union County, he was elected sheriff in 1827.[3]

Her paternal great-great-grandfather, James Cole (Kool, Kohl) was born in Holland and was among the Dutch Protestants who moved to

America in the 1600s after they had come into conflict with Catholic Spain, whose possession Holland was at the time. Her paternal great-grandfather, Benjamin Cole, was an officer in the Revolutionary War. His son, Benjamin, a private in the Revolutionary War, was killed in the War of 1812. Another son, James, was Nellie's grandfather. Her father, P. B. Cole, was born in Columbus, Ohio, in 1815. His parents, who had come from the East, first settled near Columbus, and then moved to nearby Delaware County, Ohio, where young P. B. Cole helped clear land for their new home.[4] Six decades before the Coles and the Fairbankses had arrived in the new state of Ohio, the commanding general of their Revolutionary War ancestors had been to the Ohio Territory. "History first noticed George Washington in 1753, as a daring and resourceful twenty-one-year-old messenger," historian Joseph Ellis wrote, "sent on a dangerous mission into the American wilderness … that vast region west of the Blue Ridge Mountains and south of the Great Lakes that Virginians called the Ohio Country." The letter he carried heralded the beginning of the French and Indian War.[5] The journey west was Washington's first military service. His troops in the later American Revolution—and the women who stood by them, just as Martha Washington stood by General Washington—would be the heroes and heroines of Cornelia Cole Fairbanks for the rest of her life.

Chapter Seven

Political Foremothers

Delegates were gathering in hotel lobbies to exchange the latest word from their candidate's caucuses and state meetings. The national convention would begin the next day. The leading candidates for president were a descendant of an old, distinguished Maryland Family, now prominent in New York City, and a current vice president, associated with newly wealthy Midwestern lawyers. Not to be counted out was a candidate involved in the engineering feat of constructing the Brooklyn Bridge. This was the closest women could come to being delegates to a national political convention in the United States in 1901. It was the annual Continental Congress of the Daughters of the American Revolution (DAR), one of the largest of the recently formed national women's organizations in the country and the only national society of women recognized by the United States Congress, which had granted it a charter in 1896. The *Washington Post,* describing these congresses early in the twentieth century, pointed out that Republican and Democratic parties on the eve of a nominating convention had no more maneuvering for position than did DAR delegates on the eve of their election of a national president. Members of the organization, who designated national officers with the appellation "general," considered their president general to be the female equivalent of the president of the United States.[1] National newspapers covered their conventions as they did those of Democrats and Republicans.[2,3] The members were prepared. Their leaders were experts in parliamentary procedure, and they were ready for what was usually a hotly fought election. The contest in 1901 was expected to be as vigorous as ever—and it was.

Cornelia Cole Fairbanks, of Indianapolis, Indiana, and Washington, D.C., had support from around the country, especially in the Midwest and West. She was energetic, capable, and tactful. Mrs. Fairbanks not only had many qualities of leadership, including good executive ability, but also had a very charming personality.

Emily Ritchie McLean of New York City, an orator of note and a member of several prominent clubs, was a college graduate, had taken post-graduate courses in history, and was currently active in the Society of Historical Research. She was a charter member of the DAR when it was formed ten years earlier and had been state regent for the New York Chapter and a delegate to the Congress for six years. Her husband was a well-respected lawyer in New York City. Emily Warren Roebling, of New Jersey, was the wife of the builder of the Brooklyn Bridge. She had earned a law degree and had been involved as her husband planned his monumental engineering work. When he was disabled by caisson disease, she took over much of the planning of construction. She was national vice president of the women's club Sorosis and a national vice president of the DAR. There were votes pledged to her, but Mrs. Roebling, who was a few years older than the other two candidates, was kept away from this Continental Congress by ill health.

None of these women, no matter their accomplishments, would have been allowed to vote in national or most state and local elections at the time. None of the three candidates in 1901 lived to see national woman suffrage in 1920.

On February 20, just before the 1901 election, the *New York Times* reported that the current president general, Mrs. Daniel Manning, was seen as being in favor of Mrs. Fairbanks, based on remarks she had recently made about the desirability of having a national person for president general. Her comments were seen by some as a declaration of her official right to dictate to the convention. Resistance to this added "piquancy to a rather animated canvass," as the *Times* phrased it. Mrs. McLean's supporters insisted that the incumbent could not select a successor, but rather that each president general must win on her own merits and political skill.

A major source of disagreement in this and later elections revolved around the Washington, D.C., chapters and the New York City chapter. Some of the members of the National Board, which met in Washington, and other members saw it as important that the four previous presidents general had each had a husband prominent in national politics: one a president of the United States, one a vice president, and two who were members of presidential cabinets. Cornelia Fairbanks was seen as being allied with supporters of the view that the president general should be a "national" woman. She was the wife of Senator Charles Warren Fairbanks, of Indiana, and a member of the National Board of the DAR.

One of Mrs. McLean's supporters redefined "national" woman— not as the wife of a man in national political office—but as a woman on a national platform, known for her own talents from "Maine to Texas, from California to Massachusetts."[4] The DAR had participated in an exposition in Paris and in the unveiling of monuments to George Washington and the Marquis de Lafayette there. It had sent a message of condolence to King Edward of England on the death of his mother, Queen Victoria. International recognition of the society contributed to the feeling that it was no longer necessary for the president general to be the wife of an American with an official national position.[5] Mrs. McLean was a descendant of an old, distinguished Maryland family. Her husband was a respected member of the New York City bar. It would have been most frustrating if her Revolutionary patriot ancestors, her charter membership in the DAR, and her regency of the New York City chapter were not sufficient to be elected president general—just because her husband was not prominent in national politics.

Mrs. Fairbanks might have also felt frustrated in that she, too, had qualifications other than being married to a senator. When she moved to Washington in 1897 with her newly elected husband, she was already active in the national DAR. Although she had the requisite prominent husband, she had more. Historian Francesca Morgan noted that Mrs. Fairbanks, a college graduate, had founded the first literary club for women in Indianapolis and had been the first woman appointed to the Indiana State Board of Charities. In 1900, she had been elected a director of the giant General Federation of Women's Clubs.[6] She was representative of the transition of the role of president general of the DAR from the wife of a national politician ("Mrs. Senator" Fairbanks) to that of a woman elected in her own right (Cornelia Cole Fairbanks). But it didn't seem that way to some of the delegates at the Tenth Continental Congress. The debate about a woman connected by marriage to the national government—the only way a woman could be connected to it at the time—versus a representative of local and state chapters is reminiscent of the long-running debate in the Congress of the Unites States over a strong federal government versus the rights of the several states. In the DAR contest, those favoring more influence for local groups phrased their campaign in terms of "no taxation [DAR dues] without representation." Their opponents felt that all members were represented in the national congress as it was, through their state and local chapter regents who were delegates.

Members of the DAR identified with early settlers. Membership required an ancestor who had fought in the Revolutionary War. The New York City versus Washington, D.C., fight might well have reflected different perceptions of who really did represent the founders of the country. New York City had been settled in the early seventeenth century. The District of Columbia was not established until the late eighteenth century and, of course, currently was home to representatives from all the Midwestern, less settled states so recently frontier territory. It was important to Midwesterners and others from states with even newer statehood to establish that they, too, had ancestry among the founders of the Republic. Three of the previous four presidents general had been Midwesterners, two from Indiana and one from Illinois. Easterners, on the other hand, were from states that had been the original thirteen colonies and literally lived on the ground where most of the battles of the American Revolution had been fought. They certainly had claim to national office in the DAR.

At a more personal level was a long-standing conflict of a type not uncommon between politicians of either gender—for example, Charles Fairbanks and Albert Beveridge. Candidate McLean and retiring President General Manning had been opponents in the previous election for president general that Mrs. Manning had won.[7] She was from Albany, New York, and was the second wife of Daniel Manning.[8] Her husband had been President Grover Cleveland's secretary of the treasury until Manning died in 1887. The controversy about qualifications for president general that pitted the national politician's wife versus the individual in her own right was no longer a clear dichotomy as exemplified by Mrs. Fairbanks. But this controversy was the backdrop in 1901. Nominating sessions of the Congress documented in detailed minutes in DAR archives[9] opened with Miss Batcheller:

"We, the State Regent and Chapter Regents of New Jersey, desire to present to you the name of our nominee for the next President General of the Daughters of the American Revolution. We protest against the creation of any clan of office-holders or of political position. (Applause.) … We affirm, therefore, that the possession in political life of family or ancestry should not be weighed for or against any candidate … We offer as this ideal woman one … who has the brains, the heart and the special gifts, honor, wisdom, knowledge, charity that fit her for this exalted position. In consideration of these essential qualifications … we ask the support of all the members of the Society for … Mrs. Washington Augustus Roebling, an international as well as national woman, who has made her own reputation." (Prolonged applause.)

The Delaware delegation unanimously seconded the nomination of Mrs. Roebling.

Next, Mrs. James M. Fowler of Indiana spoke:

"Madam President and Members of the Tenth Continental Congress: In selecting a President General, the Daughters of the American Revolution have never made a mistake … this large and influential Society of the Daughters needs at its head a wise, conservative and acceptable woman. The name I have to place in nomination today for President General is of a woman who possesses all these qualities in the highest sense of the word. She is wise in that she knows *when* to speak. She is conservative to a degree. She is acceptable not only on account of her long line of Revolutionary and Colonial ancestry, but because of her charming personality, her cordial manner; she is acceptable because of her individuality in thought and in action; she is acceptable because having worked upon the National Board for three years, she has been brought into close touch with work of this Board, of this Society … I have the honor to place in nomination … Mrs. Charles W. Fairbanks, of Indiana." (Prolonged applause and cheering.)

The nomination was seconded by the State Regent of New York and delegations from Ohio, Maryland, South Carolina, Oregon, Vermont, and Pennsylvania. Mrs. Fairbanks's own chapter, the Caroline Scott Harrison Chapter of Indianapolis, as well as various individuals, provided additional seconds.

Mrs. Morgan, of Georgia, then rose to speak:

"Madam President, Members of the National Board and Daughters of the American Revolution: I have the two-fold honor today of speaking for the Daughters in Georgia and of putting nomination for the position of President General, National Society Daughters of the American Revolution, a woman whose fitness for the office is so apparent, by reason of her marked ability, her graciousness and tact, her knowledge of parliamentary law (Applause.), her fund of resources, her acknowledged genius for leadership, and over all and above all, for her long, patient and distinguished services to our great Society. (Applause.) ... Mrs. McLean is so well known to you that she needs no eulogy, that you have seen her here year after year since the foundation of our Society, that you are familiar with her clear, resonant tones, coming to the rescue of the Congress in solving some knotty parliamentary problems ... you have grown to lean upon her calm, judicial mind, to shape the settlement of questions of law and equity, of right and privilege—in short, ... Mrs. McLean's name is a familiar sound to our general membership from the granite hills of New England to the Savannahs of the South, from ocean to ocean."

The nomination was seconded by Michigan, New Hampshire, the Buffalo Chapter, the Baron Steuben Chapter of New York, the Mohegan Chapter of New York, the Johnstown Chapter of New York, the New York City Chapter, the Frederick Chapter of Maryland, the Dorothy Ripley Chapter of Connecticut, and the George Rogers Clark

Chapter of Oak Park, Illinois. Fittingly, many individuals spoke for Mrs. McLean, some arguing eloquently against the necessity of electing a woman whose husband was prominent in national politics.

Clearly these women were ready for campaigns and conventions of national political parties! But the New Woman of the twentieth century wasn't there yet. Balloting took place into the evening, and tellers stayed up until five o'clock the next morning tallying votes. At the session of the Continental Congress later that morning, among great anticipation, Mrs. Park rose to give the teller's report of election results: "The official report of the Tellers' committee is: The number of votes cast, 584; necessary to elect, 293; Mrs. Fairbanks, for President General received 333." (There was prolonged applause and cheers, and excitement on the floor, waving of handkerchiefs, etc.) President General Manning requested quiet until the announcement was complete. Mrs. Park continued: "Mrs. Donald McLean received 208 votes; (Great applause.), one ballot rejected. Mrs. Roebling, 42 votes." (Applause.)

Controversy between Mrs. Manning and Mrs. McLean continued, whatever Mrs. Fairbanks might have thought about it. Mrs. Fowler's comment in nominating Mrs. Fairbanks, "She is wise in that she knows *when* to speak," was possibly intended to set Mrs. Fairbanks apart from the controversy. She apparently did not speak publicly about it.

After election results were announced, a member moved that a vote of thanks be given to tellers and inspectors who had stayed up most of the night counting votes. Then Mrs. McLean rose to request a grant of personal privilege. She addressed Mrs. Fairbanks who directed her to Mrs. Manning who was still presiding officially, as Mrs. McLean was aware. Mrs. Manning granted the privilege.

Mrs. McLean continued, "I merely wish to say ... that in acknowledging the election of our President General—and my relations with her, while slight, have always been agreeable—I have never sullied my self-respect by one word of aught but respect for her. (Applause.) I wish to say now that I desire to thank personally and officially every one of the loyal and devoted friends who have been my friends here ... And I further wish to say, and to beg the President General duly elected—and I am sure that she will grant me this second favor, although not technically in the Chair—I beg the President General to use her great office to protect the members of her organization (hisses) from calumny."

Mrs. McLean was referring to hotly contested debates in caucuses, and information circulated among delegates, between her supporters and her opponents. Characteristic of any political convention, each side had accused the other of salacious comments and unfair tactics. Newspapers of the time carried reports, uncomplimentary or even sexist, about conflicts within the DAR.[10] During the ensuing discussion, there were cries of "Time!" "Out of order!" "Order of the day!" and the like.

Mrs. McLean then said, "Madam President and Madam Chairman: I think that the position I have taken beside this newly elected President, should entitle me simply to one or two statements which reflect on no one, but do assist me."

President General Manning ruled, "The Chair has granted Mrs. McLean ten minutes. The House has granted Mrs. McLean ten minutes. She has a right to it." (Applause.)

Mrs. McLean continued, "I shall consume the rest of that ten minutes only in this. Believe me, I am as incapable of doing aught to unjustly or unrightly prevent the proper election by a majority, of any woman who this Congress nominated, as I am incapable of anything else which I believe absolutely to be wrong." (Applause.)

Clearly these women were ready to run for national office and to debate on the floor of the Congress of the United States! But the New Woman wasn't there yet.

President General Manning then introduced Mrs. Fairbanks who, after prolonged applause and cheering, said:

"Madame President, Daughters of the Tenth Continental Congress assembled here in convention, I greet you. I thank you for the honor which you have conferred upon me, the highest one in your power to bestow. I thank you who have so loyally attached yourselves to my fortunes. Words may but feebly express my affectionate appreciation of your loyalty, your unswerving fidelity, but be assured that the tenderest recollections of you and your labors shall remain forever upon my memory and in my heart. (Applause.) For those who have opposed me I have the kindest thoughts, and thank them for their courteous treatment of me during our campaign. (Applause.) I now call upon you most cordially to join in carrying out the grand designs which brought our Society into being. (Applause.) Let us all forget our differences of opinion which belonged to yesterday, but press on to the high calling marked out for us by the big-brained, far-seeing, noble-hearted founders of our National Society. Heaven bless them, and give them length of days, prosperity, and peace. We have wonderfully momentous duties devolving upon us; for the National Society of Daughters of the American Revolution is like an elder daughter of the republic, for we labor under the charter of the United States government; hence it behooves us most seriously to cherish, maintain, and extend the institutions of American freedom, to foster true patriotism, and love of country, and to aid in securing for mankind all the blessings of liberty. (Applause.)

"Compared to these ideas how petty are minor differences of opinion concerning management. How much more pitiful are thoughts of personal aggrandizement. Let us banish such poor ideas, and cherish those others which are somewhat akin to divine thoughts.

"Let us remember to mark all those historic spots rendered illustrious and sacred by the suffering, blood, devotion, and patriotism of our Revolutionary heroes. Let us not forget to seek the protection of the United States Congress against the sacrilegious and desecrating uses of our flag—that emblem of humanity. Let us strive to keep the National Society of the Daughters of the American Revolution up to a high standard of splendid achievements.

"Again thanking you for the distinguished consideration with which you have listened to me, I hope that good fortune will attend you all on your homeward journeys, and that happiness and health will attend you in all your homes. Au Revoir!"

Mrs. Fairbanks was divorcing herself from "minor differences of opinion concerning management"—the controversy that had been present throughout the Congress. She was indirectly defining her role as a mediator among factions in order to keep the society "up to a high standard of splendid achievement," as she would do during the four years of her presidency. On a broader scale, an "elder daughter of the republic," laboring "under the charter of the United States government," while respectfully deferential to the all male executive, legislative, and judicial branches of the time, might well be contemplating the possibility of women serving in the executive, legislative, and judicial branches in the future. Mrs. Fairbanks believed that women should vote and take an active part in politics.[11]

Chapter Eight

Reins of Government Well in Hand

President General Fairbanks, presiding for the first time at the Continental Congress in 1902, was crisp, courteous, knowledgeable, and to the point: she asked members to send every motion "up to the desk in writing before it can be announced. The official reader will read the motion"; later, after an interruption by applause, she said, "The Chair requests that you refrain from applause so that the progress of business will be facilitated"; a little later, she said, "The Chair is exceedingly willing that every light shall be thrown upon this subject. The Chair declares, however, that this is not the time for that discussion at present, unless you can confine yourself closely to the resolution which has been offered"; on another matter, she said, "Madam, your motion can be presented a little later. We have now before us the motion to accept the report of the program committee"; when a member inquired how much time was left for discussion of a particular matter, she said, "We have forty-nine minutes."[1]

Many of the members were not as familiar with parliamentary proceedings as their officers. Mrs. Fairbanks frequently explained rules of procedure with kindness, courtesy, and good humor: "First I think we will take up the amendments in the order in which they are proposed, and then whatever you have regarding that subject you can bring forward. We are going to proceed to the consideration of amendments in the order in which they are printed. The official reader will please read the first one. The Chair will rule that the official reader may read the article of the constitution or of the by-laws which is to be amended, and then read the article as it will be when it is amended. It, therefore, is very necessary for you to keep quiet and listen attentively, as these are important considerations."[2] There were times, however, that it was necessary for her to say, "Madam, take your seat. You are out of order." And she did so, graciously but firmly.[3]

Mrs. McLean's clear resonant tones regarding parliamentary proceedings continued as in previous Continental Congresses:

President Fairbanks: "Those in favor of this amendment of Miss Miller in regard to taking the program *seriatim,* and taking recesses instead of adjourning, will please signify it by saying 'aye'; those opposed, 'no.' The 'ayes' seem to have it. (After a pause.) The 'ayes' have it and it is so ordered. The question is now upon the adoption of the motion to accept the report of the program committee as amended. The official reader—"

Mrs. McLean: "A question of information. There have been two terms used in relation to the program; one of them is the 'acceptance' of the report, and the other is the 'adoption' of the report. I understand that occasionally on the floor of this house there has been a difference made between those two terms. Is there a difference now?"

President Fairbanks: "According to Robert's rules of order 'accept' and 'adopt' are synonymous."

Mrs. McLean: "That is the point of information on which I wished your ruling. Then, in adopting this report, we adopt its every suggestion."

President Fairbanks: "As amended."

Mrs. McLean: "Then, may I ask the Chair to rule on this point. Taking a recess instead of an adjournment, I think, means simply that after taking a recess at five o'clock this afternoon, when we come together in the morning, we proceed with the business which was before us at five o'clock rather than to take up [tomorrow] morning's business."

President Fairbanks: "That is the idea."

Mrs. McLean: "Then, if the amendments come before us this afternoon for only five minutes, when we come together in the morning we proceed with them rather than with the morning's program."

President Fairbanks: "That is the idea."[4]

A woman columnist wrote of Mrs. Fairbanks, "Not a dissenting voice is heard as to the sweet graciousness of her manner, and the wise, fair judgment of her rulings. She placates without losing a jot of control, and considers the right of each member to be heard. She never appears to be favoring one side more than another. It would be impossible to know on which side her sympathies were by the way she presides and, however great the turmoil, keeps the reins of government well in hand. She has a level head and an amiable disposition, two invincible traits in a presiding officer."[5] Another columnist thought, "Mrs. Fairbanks is always radiant with good humor. She is not easily disturbed, and can carry off a difficult situation that may arise with a nonchalance that is the envy of all her friends. The ability to do this comes not only from good nature, but from seeing life in its proper lines and knowing how to distinguish between the essentially tragic and the really trivial things of life."[6]

The ability to carry off a difficult situation with nonchalance was the outward presence of a woman who had written privately to her husband just a few years before, "you know I am in the habit of thinking I have mortal illness when I feel a little under the weather," and who had referred to her "worrisome nature ... I know not why it is, but I am constantly bothering myself about something or one or all of [the family and children]."[7] Whatever the extent of an underlying worrisome nature in the context of raising her young children in the 1880s and 1890s, in 1901 she was certainly able to cope with it well.

Mrs. Mary Lockwood, a DAR founder, wrote, "When Mrs. Fairbanks was elected President General those who like to see good chairmanship were delighted at the prospect of having so accomplished a presiding officer, nor were they disappointed. While strictly parliamentary in her rulings, she, through intuition and a fine womanly tact, knew when to 'yield a point' as well as her distinguished husband. She may be said to be one of the 'New Women,' having had much valuable all-round experience in Women's Clubs."[8]

Mrs. Fairbanks was the first president general to set up an office at headquarters, and she reorganized the national office. She was in Washington during most of the year except for the summer recesses of Congress when she and her family returned to Indianapolis. In Washington, she would usually be in her office for several hours a day, devoting herself to the business of the organization. Adding to her popularity was her "democratic and sympathetic way of greeting every Daughter, be she Vice President or one of the working corps at headquarters ... whom she always recognized as being as worthy of consideration as herself."[9] After it was reported to the national group in 1902 that a few chapters had been educating immigrants about citizenship, by 1904 there was a Committee on Patriotic Education supplied with space and clerical personnel at national headquarters.[10] Results of the president general's organizing capabilities and ability to inspire others soon became apparent. During her four years as president general from 1901 to 1905, the number of chapters of the society increased from 567 to 740 and membership from just over 35,000 to almost 52,000, a 50 percent increase.[11] In order to deal with some of the kinds of dissention within the organization that had become so apparent in 1901, Mrs. Fairbanks was empowered by the delegates in 1903 to form a committee to develop a code of ethics. Matters needing investigation would be referred to this committee which could then establish the facts during the year and make recommendations to the annual meeting of the Continental Congress, reducing the time consumed in discussion on the floor.[12] For example, an investigating committee in 1904 gave a report about conflicts in the Philadelphia chapter. During the 1901 Congress, there had been a simmering fight in the Philadelphia delegation between two members competing for DAR office, one of whom had accused the other of defects of character and was in turn being sued by the accused. Thanks to the report of the ethics committee in 1904, "at one of the stormiest sessions in its history, the thirteenth annual congress of the Daughters of the American Revolution today adopted a report which vindicates Miss Harriet Baird Huey. The report ... virtually clears Miss Baird Huey from all aspersions on her character."[13]

The new president general opened the 1902 Continental Congress, held in an auditorium at Fifteenth Street and Pennsylvania Avenue:

"Members of the Eleventh Continental Congress: It is my most valued pleasure to welcome you to the capital of your country, to the national home of the Daughters of the American Revolution, to your great annual council.

"I bid you welcome to our homes and the best therein, and I would that time and circumstance would permit you each to join us at our firesides where we might listen to the story of your growth and vicissitudes as chapters, of your labors already performed for the attainment of the significant objects of your organization—the plans you have made to preserve the spirit of liberty which animated the men and women of the Revolution and to foster patriotism. I welcome you to these halls where, for a brief portion of time, you will consider questions relating to the usefulness, the welfare and honor of your great society …

"Of the many important questions to be discussed by the Eleventh Continental Congress, none is of more paramount significance and none has awakened more widespread interest than the amendment relating to the reduction of representation. (Prolonged applause.)

"Upon one side is presented the old and oft-debated declaration that 'taxation without representation is tyranny.' Upon the other hand, the friends of this measure claim that there is no intention that there should be taxation without representation because whatever measure is adopted it will surely be one which has in view a full representation of the National Society in the Continental Congress. (Applause.) It is also stated that the rapidly increasing growth of our society is such that perhaps by another year or two, at the present rate of representation there could not be found an audience room adequately to accommodate our delegates. It is claimed that should there be erected an auditorium vast enough in size to seat thousands of delegates who would later come to the Continental Congress (for there is no reason to doubt that by two decades more the Society may number one hundred thousand members). (Applause.) Therefore in a Congress, at the present rate of representation, it is feared that there would be difficulty in the voice of any one speaker being heard [in a day before microphones]. It is also contended that great numbers interfere with the transaction of business; so it seems, while there is upon one side a misapprehension of the great statement which always challenges the admiration of every American, 'taxation without representation is tyranny,' there is upon the other side a consideration of space, of strength of voice, of facility in the transaction of business and the fact that the representation will still be ample, and far more forcible, because concentrated. It remains with you, Daughters of the American Revolution, assembled here in Congress, carefully to deliberate and wisely to decide this great question so deeply affecting the practical working of our Society."[14]

She had laid out concisely the disagreement between those proposing no diminution in the number of delegates and those who felt that there should be fewer delegates, for example, by having a delegation selected by a majority of chapters in a state rather than by having delegates from each chapter. Ultimately, she left it up to the delegates themselves "carefully to deliberate and wisely to decide." She had also implied a compromise that was dear to her heart—build a hall with an auditorium that would accommodate a large number of delegates—the proposed Memorial Continental Hall. Building the Memorial Hall would be the major project of her presidency and that for which she is remembered by the DAR today. She was going to waste no time in getting the job done. The matter of reduction in the number of delegates was hotly debated from many viewpoints. President General Fairbanks requested "that this debate be divided ... that the speakers shall alternate, first a speaker on one side and then one on the other side," and she held the delegates to that request until all had spoken.[15] Many versions of the amendment to reduce the number of delegates were proposed. Mrs. McLean, supported by many, objected that "[i]f adopted [the amendment] will reduce the representation, and therefore the size of the congress, and will reduce it how? By barring absolutely from the floor of this congress the great majority of its members, the life blood of the organization, the chapters."[16] Ultimately, the amendment to reduce the number of delegates was defeated.

On another controversial matter, President General Fairbanks carefully wended her way among pro and con comments about changes in dues, what portion of dues should go to the national office, what to do with surpluses in the budget, and disbursement of a fund for Memorial Continental Hall that had been increasing for a decade through annual contributions and accrued interest.[17] Discussing the issues of dues and the budget, Mrs. McLean brought up local chapters' versus national officers' concerns:

"It is only a question of how much money comes here and how much money is reserved. Shall chapters which exist all over the country and manifestly do all the local historical work of the country, send one-half of their entire income to the central organization, or shall they retain three-fourths of the annual income to provide for their responsible and patriotic work throughout the whole year. That is the question, and that is the principle involved. Every one of us, so far as I know, is loyal to the interests of Continental Hall. It has been one of the objects of this Society from its birth … It is the object of our national work. It is not the object of our local work."[18] Finally, a compromise was reached on how to distribute funds, nationally and locally, including allocation of funds for the planned Memorial Constitutional Hall.

One of many issues on which there was much less disagreement was a request by the Spirit of Liberty chapter of Salt Lake City for a vote against polygamy. They expressed support of many Mormon people "who are trying to do right … the greatest kindness to do them is to rebuke this evil." The Continental Congress voted that "[n]o one who is polygamist, a descendant of a polygamist, or sympathetic to polygamy be a member" of the DAR. Delegates believed that they were "[s]peaking up for American womanhood."[19]

Having participated in planning and financing a building for women in a state capital, Indianapolis, President General Fairbanks was well on her way to building a prominent building, planned and financed by women, in the nation's capital. It would be near the White House and other public buildings and not easily overlooked. The beautiful structure would honor ordinary men and women whose labors had built the nation. On a particularly inclement night, Mrs. Fairbanks complimented the delegates on braving the storm through flooded streets in their long dresses and added, "Washington crossed the Delaware when the river was full of floating ice, and you ladies must not be backward in emulating his example. If he crossed the Delaware, you can certainly cross a pavement from your carriage." Her comments were greeted with tremendous applause. After giving the chair to a vice president, she delivered a stirring address urging the purchase of land for the memorial hall. Within a few minutes, almost eight thousand dollars had been raised.[20]

Plans for Continental Memorial Hall developed rapidly in nine committee meetings during Mrs. Fairbanks's first year as president general. During discussion in the following Congress, Mrs. McLean again suggested caution:

"I would suggest that that is a very large thing for this body to consider which has stirred up Washington a great deal, and I understand, the United States Congress, the great plan for the beautification of the city of Washington. We certainly have read and heard a great deal of it during the last year. It would seem wise that if this body is to build an everlasting memorial to the Heroes of the Revolution that they should be in line with this wonderful beautification of this city. Let us then not too hastily procure a site for fear that if the committee appointed by the Congress of the United States should select a different route of beautification we might be outside the line, and in addition if they should decide that we are in the line they might prefer to put something else there where our site would. I do not suppose it would, but all things are possible ...

"Therefore would it not be wise before actually considering and agreeing upon a site to consult whatever committee is appointed by the United States Congress looking toward the permanent beautification of this great city?"[21]

The Washington versus New York City rivalry remained not far below the surface. Mrs. McLean seemed to be calling attention to Mrs. Fairbanks's position in official Washington society while at the same time possibly implying that the wishes of the president general might not be consonant with those of her senator husband's colleagues. Mrs. Fairbanks's husband was on the Committee on Public Buildings and Grounds of the United States Senate. The final vote on the measure approved the site proposed by the committee.

The following year, 1903, President General Fairbanks addressed the annual Continental Congress:

"The Daughters of the American Revolution have before them at present one of the most absorbing works which they have ever undertaken. It is composite in its nature, being at once a memorial monument and the administrative building of the society which erects it. It is to evince that gratitude which we owe to those who carved our country from mountains, wilderness and desert waste, which offered opportunity, home and happiness, to all who came hither inspired with a resolve to become worthy American citizens. The fathers and mothers of the Revolution builded, suffered and conquered, had their toilsome but glorious day, and passed to their rest. It is now the duty of their descendants inspired with that noblest sentiment—gratitude—to raise a testimonial of appreciation to their virtues. Let it have so beautifully, yet so distinctly, inscribed upon its portals and upon its majestic columns the story of the devotion to liberty that even the wayfarer may read and understand it. (Applause.) This shall be of practical usefulness as well as of reverence and remembrance. From the lessons derived from this monument dedicated to the memory of patriots, may there flow, like rivers to the sea, through all humanity enriching streams of generous resolves for country and liberty, undaunted purpose to emulate the patriotic zeal, the unselfish devotion of the Revolutionary heroes. (Applause.)"[22]

Chapter Nine

Building a National Audience

Mrs. Fairbanks's speaking engagements around the country for the next four years began soon after her election in 1901. First, she attended meetings of the Board of Directors of the General Federation of Women's Clubs, which met in Washington later in February. Then she represented the national DAR at the opening of the American Hall of Fame in New York City on Memorial Day.[1] She addressed DAR members at the Pan-American Exposition in Buffalo, where a reception was given in her honor.[2] New York state members, giving several receptions, managed to arrange invitations, guest lists, and speakers in order to deal with the long-running competition between the two New Yorkers, Mrs. Manning of Albany and Mrs. McLean of New York City.[3] The exposition in Buffalo would play a momentous role in the life of Charles and Cornelia Fairbanks. It was there that their good friend President McKinley was assassinated in September 1901 by anarchist Leon Czolgosz. Mrs. Fairbanks gave a speech to the Chicago DAR the following month pleading, "Let us try to teach all with whom we come in contact that … American institutions must be upheld. Let us instruct and teach those who come to this land of freedom and liberty that there is a great difference between liberty and license … they must learn to respect the rights of others; let us teach them the significance of the flag. If we succeed in this we shall never again see the red rag of anarchy in our streets. It is the grand mission of this society to teach liberty."[4]

During her busy travels, she was scheduled to visit the Georgia DAR in Atlanta, but sent a telegram to them that she had been called to Marysville, Ohio, because of a death in the family.[5] Her eldest brother, Ulysses, had been practicing law in Rushville, Indiana, at the time of his sudden death in November 1901. At home in Washington, Nellie's youngest son, fifteen-year-old Robert, described in his diary the intersecting events of his parents' lives and his uncle's death: "Sun. Nov. 17, Mama had callers, or dictated letters, or had her hair dressed almost all day … Mama is writing her speech, which she delivers in Georgia. She read it to me just before dinner. It's all right." The next day, he wrote, "Mama was gone but there was a telegram from Papa saying he would be here tonight." After the senator arrived home, he and Robert spent the evening together. The following day, he wrote, "A little while after dinner, a telegram came, saying that Uncle Lyss died this morning. Mama telegraphed that she wanted to go there as fast possible. Papa tried to make arrangements."[6] In her opening address to the 1903 Continental Congress, Mrs. Fairbanks reported that she "had the very great pleasure and advantage of paying visits to a number of state conferences … [observing] the zeal and interest of the Daughters in these widely separate localities." There were very many that the president general "might have visited had there been more days at her command. It is with sincere regret that she failed in accepting the very kind and urgent invitations from many states."[7]

In a speech delivered to the State DAR after she had visited the South Carolina Inter-State and West Indian Exposition, Mrs. Fairbanks said:

"I have been delighted and interested with the South Carolina Inter-State and West Indian Exposition, which within a few hours I have had the pleasure of visiting, where I have moved through the halls of that old Colonial home, dedicated to the work of the woman's department of this exposition. I have viewed with deepest interest the exhibit which these public spirited women of your state have placed there …

"Now, may I add I am especially pleased to be the guest of the Daughters of the American Revolution of this commonwealth, who come of that illustrious line of patriots who so effectively aided in gaining independence and establishing our country upon a secure basis. Of all the thirteen states which engaged in the most memorable of all wars, in contending for the welfare not only of home and native land, but as it transpired, also for the happiness of all the world, no state was more zealous in its patriotism, more splendid in the valor of its soldiers, none more noted for the patriotic aid and endurance of its splendid daughters, none which gave more soldiers for the prosecution of the war, than did the brave state of South Carolina. That conduct is an inspiration to all mankind, more especially for us, who have for our object all the reasons for the existence of our purely patriotic society, the thought to keep fresh in memory the spirit of liberty which animated both the men and the women of the Revolution and to rescue from oblivion and neglect the records of those whose valor and whose fortitude have been less noted than their merits demanded."

Her knowledge of history was apparent in detailed references to many local Revolutionary War heroes, both well known and relatively unknown, women as well as men. She continued:

"The decided stand the women of South Carolina took in the Revolution cheered the sometimes faint hearts of the soldiers. They knew they had behind them, in these women, a tower of strength—a world of patriotic love, anxious solicitude and confidence. They cheered the soldiers to the front and bound up the wounds they suffered in the battles. They encouraged them to give time, money, and life, if needful, and were ever ready to extend the hand of friendship and to cheer and sustain those of weaker heart and strength. As we read of these thrilling memories of Revolutionary times there rises before us a procession of dainty and gracious figures, of strong hearts and resolved patriotism … the influence of women, so powerful an agent during the progress of the Revolutionary War, was equally exercised afterward in restoring healthful tone and vigor to society …

"After contemplating this brief recital of the powers of patriotism, of the heroism, the suffering, trials and final triumphs of our Revolutionary forefathers and foremothers, it is becoming for a great patriotic society profoundly to reflect upon commemorating these illustrious deeds of the illustrious patriots—fittingly to commemorate them by a grand memorial …

"I trust that the Daughters of the American Revolution from all over this land, may feel it their pleasure—their bounden duty—their privilege to dedicate themselves to this noble work, now before our society. Let us not forget to thus preserve the spirit of those who contended for the principle, the eternal principle of right and justice."[8]

She reported on another visit to chapters in a letter to the editor of the NSDAR *American Monthly Magazine.*

"In recalling to you a very delightful visit which it was my good fortune recently to make, I feel that I would like you … to share with me, in retrospect, some of the pleasures which were mine in the fleeting glimpse of the Bazaar at Boston given for the noble purpose of aiding Memorial Continental Fund.

"It was my intention to have arrived at the opening of this patriotic movement; but I did not reckon with railroad travel, and the results of

New England winters ... it was my misfortune to arrive at five minutes past eleven. However, this belated arrival did not prevent a visit on the morrow to the scene organized and made interesting by the patriotic Daughters of Massachusetts.

"The Bazaar was held at Copley Hall; a name which brings to us memories of one of the greatest artists who depicted so many fair women and brave men of the Revolutionary period.

"On entering this hall ... among the first objects which appeared with most distinctness before us, was a large company of gentle dames, arrayed in Colonial costume, with powdered hair and brocaded gowns, busily offering their wares for sale ... for the Continental Hall project." A "Real Daughter," whose father had fought at Lexington and Concord and who was herself now aged ninety-nine years was in attendance.

Mrs. Fairbanks mentioned the chapters and individuals involved and described the serving of beverages of the Colonial period for which a recipe book could be purchased, a fortune telling booth, and displays of a box rescued when thrown overboard at the Boston Tea Party and other relics of the period. One Daughter donated priceless pieces of china for sale because she had "no money to give to this cause." Mrs. Fairbanks was "happy to say that the Daughters of Massachusetts have deemed it a pleasure and a privilege to compensate this lady for her generosity." In addition to handkerchiefs, sachets, "delicious viands," and other items for sale, there were speeches, musical performances, and other entertainments. Three thousand four hundred dollars was raised—a handsome sum a century ago.[9]

On another occasion, dedicating a bronze tablet to the memory of French General Lafayette in Rockville, Connecticut, she said:

"It is with sincere pleasure that I meet the citizens of Rockville and the Daughters of the American Revolution united in gracious consideration of the memory and fame of one of our foreign allies during the War for Independence ... it is fitting that [the tablet] bear the name of the buoyant young Frenchman who came, bringing with him the prestige of his position and nation, the hope which inspired our devoted Washington and his heroic army to renewed vigor in the war, which with its close finally brought into the world, into the family of nations an undoubted haven for the downtrodden."[10]

Four days later in Syracuse, New York, celebrating Bunker Hill Day with the dedication of a bronze plaque, Mrs. Fairbanks declaimed:

"The great society of patriotic women which I have the honor to represent feels the deepest interest in occasions such as this, wherein its members may show their fond appreciation of the sacrifices and work of the great army of the Revolution, the women as well as the men, who gave their substance, devoted their lives that their homes and sanctuaries might be free ... the date [battle of Bunker Hill] when those undisciplined but sturdy, determined, old-time sons of the American Revolution struck mighty blows for freedom 'gainst fearful odds' even the numerous, well-equipped, imperious forces of old England. But they performed yeomen's service not only for God and native land, but in so doing made here a haven for the liberty-loving and oppressed throughout the whole world."[11]

Historic preservation by women's organizations, important both for understanding the history of the nation and for understanding the history of American women, has been the subject of recent research. Barbara Howe pointed out that the DAR was the first national organization to protect historic sites in the United States, working "through local chapters and state societies. Its objectives included 'the acquisition and protection of historical spots, and the erection of monuments'... These plaques and monuments, although intended as commemorative, are now themselves historic resources, documenting the history of the historic preservation movement." Howe went on to describe the westward movement of veterans after the war, noting that the Caroline Scott Harrison Chapter (Cornelia Fairbanks's chapter) marked graves in Indianapolis.[12]

In 1903, the Continental Congress of the DAR recommended to the United States Congress that the historic site of Jamestown, Virginia, be protected from water erosion, restored to its original condition, and beautified. A delegation of DAR officers visited Jamestown where Mrs. Fairbanks made a speech. Full fruition of the preservation of Jamestown, including subsequent archeological discoveries, was demonstrated a century later at the Four Hundred Year celebration of the Jamestown landing in 2007. The same Continental Congress endorsed a bill in the United States House of Representatives to appropriate money for assistance in establishing a memorial at the Pilgrim Landing Site on Cape Cod, Massachusetts, a famous historic site today.[13] The DAR protested against the Park Commission's decision to destroy historic buildings like old St. John's Church in Washington and homes in several states of many who had been important in the history of the country. They supported their chapters that were working to preserve historic sites and implemented the placing of bronze plaques in sites that would honor patriots and scientists of the United States. They voted resolutions to Congress to recover the remains of the crewmen of the U.S. S. Maine which had sunk in Havana harbor in 1898 and properly bury them in Arlington National Cemetery and to return the remains of Revolutionary War naval commander John Paul Jones from France to the United States.[14] At a patriotic gathering, reported by the *Washington Evening Star,* February 15, 1902, Mrs. Fairbanks spoke of work of the DAR: "It is quite a mistake to term ours an aristocratic organization. We are aristocrats in revering our ancestors who gave us the Declaration of Independence and the Constitution of the United States, if you can possibly fashion that sentiment into a badge of aristocracy; but I fancy you will find that our pride of ancestry is not the ignoble sentiment that dominates the snobbish seeker after tarnished glory. Our pride in ancestry is the natural outgrowth of the inherited patriotic spirit that comes down to us from a long line of men who in the trenches, behind the guns, on the ships fought the fight that gave us a nation and a flag. [The DAR members were not] just gathering relics of the past. We are studying history ourselves, and we are teaching our children a broader comprehension of the history of their own country ... have done research that has revealed valuable materials, established chairs of history, founded local libraries, established prizes for students." She discussed work during the Spanish-American War when the DAR had supported nurses to care for the troops, sent supplies to the troops, and greeted them at troop trains with sandwiches and coffee on their return from the front. More recently, the DAR had established a clubhouse in Manila for soldiers fighting in the Philippines in the aftermath of the Spanish-American War.

Educational efforts of the DAR had ranged all the way from paying for lecturers on American history in colleges to establishing "in several large cities, regular courses in American history in the slums, where foreigners are addressed in the mother tongue on patriotic principles and good citizenship ... Particularly are we looking after the little foreign waifs in overcrowded cities, and gathering them into schools where they, too, are taught the first principles of a free government, and the duty they owe it ... It is in this kind of 'aristocracy' that I glory." As she was outlining the good works of the DAR around the country, she was also dealing with internal disagreements in the organization at headquarters in Washington. There was constant accusation that the Washington members were interested in using the organization for partisan politics. Such accusations were particularly pertinent because Charles Warren Fairbanks had been proposed as a candidate for the Republican nomination for president and was a candidate for nomination as vice president in 1904. Any suggestion that the DAR as an organization would back him reflected on the character of Mrs. Fairbanks as being more interested in partisan politics and personal prominence than in the principles of the patriotic organization. The previous presidents of the DAR had included two Republicans and two Democrats. Washingtonians insisted that they had never used the DAR to promote any political party or candidate. Mrs. Fairbanks was attacked in print while she was promoting the building of Continental Memorial Hall. There were accusations published around the country of fraudulent use of funds collected for the building. This provoked an authorized statement concerning the Continental Hall work, issued at DAR headquarters by the National Board. The statement objected to efforts to prevent work on the hall by misinforming members and the public about what was happening, thus diminishing contributions from chapters to the building fund. Details of relevant meetings, decisions, and expenditures were given. The report added, "It was with reluctance that the national board issued through the Associated Press a public statement yesterday. So long as the board as a body only received its perennial attack, the members felt that they could bear the strain with equanimity, but when these statements ... became personal reflections on the administration of the much-beloved president general of the society, it was felt that the time had come when even the conservative element of the society must go into print with the official records."[15]

Like Senator Fairbanks, DAR President General Fairbanks and her supporters were not unaware of the use of print media. Also, like her husband, Nellie worked skillfully behind the scenes.

In the midst of all this, she pursued her goals of continuing projects of educating young people about patriotism, commemorating historic sites around the country, and building a home for the National Society of the Daughters of the American Revolution, in Washington, D.C. "At great personal inconvenience she ... traveled about the country giving a cheering word and helping hand to any chapter calling to her for assistance, sometimes, to be sure, to meet much honorable attention by the way and achieve great distinction, but more frequently to give her time, her strength, and her means in the cause of the society she loves, and which owes its present strength and honor more to her individual efforts than to any other one force in its upbuilding."[16]

Mrs. Fairbanks's leadership was demonstrating that women's organizations could function well although the press often caricatured political disagreements in the DAR in negative terms: for example, "lady-patriots all of whom inherit the pugnacious tendencies of the original American insurgents,"[17] or "Individually they are representative American ladies; collectively they are a mob."[18]

President General Fairbanks addressed male amusement with feminist rhetoric. For example, she told the *Philadelphia Press* in late June 1902, before an Independence Day talk there, "That the busy men of this nation should look with something more than tolerance upon the work and value of women's patriotic work is the excuse for this little Fourth of July talk." In her talk, she said:

"These organizations, as it were, are merely tolerated by men. They seem to think their women folk are out of mischief when attending the meetings of a patriotic society. The newspaper world gives space to the description of their conventions with the good-natured intention of extracting amusement from the proceedings.

"The patriotic organizations of women have done much for the nation. During the past dozen years they have encouraged timely legislation to preserve the flag from abuse. They have inculcated patriotism in the young. At their suggestion the public schools have revived the presentation of object lessons in patriotism ...

"Another good work to which the women's patriotic societies have devoted themselves is the Junior Republic. Everybody knows the purpose and the good results of this work. In itself, it was essentially a feminine conception. Every mother, indeed, every woman knows that during the period that the man is a boy his instincts should be developed. Therefore, in the Junior Republic the youth of the country is given an opportunity to study and practice the virtues which will be most decorous during manhood. The youngsters are taught self-restraint, orderly obedience and acquiescence to the rules of society. They are also taught that if a wrong exists, each and every citizen of the republic should endeavor to right it and not endanger the permanence of good order by rebellion. In the Junior Republic, bright boys learn that law is wise and order necessary. The methods of proper amendment of conditions are realized and the citizen who graduates from the Junior Republic enters upon his manly life equipped as a very knight of progress. His devotion to law and his patriotism are fully developed."

She noted that women's patriotic societies had bought with their own money homes of the "revolutionary fathers," many of which "a busy nation had forgotten" and emphasized the importance of preserving that history. None of the states involved in the war was without Revolutionary War memorials. The DAR had located the few hundred surviving immediate descendents of Revolutionary War veterans and had cared for them in their old age.

Remarking that it was more than 125 years since Washington and his soldiers had achieved independence, she pointed out, "The son of a woman belonging to a patriotic society is not likely to be influenced by the sneer that we are a young nation with no traditional ideal."

She concluded, "'By our works, ye shall know us,' The flags over the schoolhouses, the Junior Republic, the ease and contentment of the last real Daughters of the Revolution, the monuments over historic spots and in memory of exemplary men, all speak most eloquently for the labors of patriotic American women."[19]

Cornelia Fairbanks was a natural for the Junior Republic—it helped poor children and taught patriotism. Leading citizens in Baltimore and nearby Washington, D.C., were becoming interested in the work of William R. George in Freeville, New York, with inner-city youth. They organized the National Junior Republic at Annapolis Junction under Maryland law in 1899 and excited interest through public meetings. A charming and gracious senator's wife prominent in prestigious Washington clubs and in national women's organizations, Cornelia Fairbanks was the obvious person to be first president of the Women's League of the National Junior Republic. Once involved, Mrs. Fairbanks kept "open house" at her home where "brilliant gatherings of the foremost representatives of Washington society were entertained and much sympathy and financial aid for the project obtained."[20] DAR women supported Junior Republics. In 1890, William R. George had opened a summer camp on family property near Freeville, New York, for boys and girls rejected by other organizations. People in the area knew George and were willing to help. He was assisted in the summer camp by a "small band of volunteers, most of them women."[21]

George firmly believed that "every normal boy, no matter how sordid the conditions into which he was born, had in him latent possibilities which, if properly fostered, could and would place him in the highest and most honorable social ranks."[22] After trial and error of various educational methods, he began a program of self-government with all the elements of executive, legislative, and judicial offices run by the boys and girls who elected their officials and developed laws for governing themselves. They learned what behaviors worked to their benefit in the context of the community. There were adults present in parental roles such as housemothers. Many Junior Republic graduates did become productive citizens in spite of their origins in street gangs.[23] Girls were later admitted to George's Junior Republic in New York, and they voted and held office in the Junior Republic before adult women in New York were able to do so in state and national elections. The National Junior Republic at Annapolis Junction was pre-eminent among the half dozen clubs established around the country using George's model. It was abandoned in 1917 during the First World War four years after Mrs. Fairbanks had died in Indianapolis.[24]

Chapter Ten

Politics Is Good Fun

One of the major victories of women in public life at the turn of the twentieth century was to achieve official participation at World's Fairs commemorating historical events. Women had demanded recognition at the Columbian Exposition in Chicago in 1893, seeking not only to "highlight but also to demand recognition for women's involvement in public life and reform throughout the 'century of women.'" A Board of Lady Managers was appointed, and the United States Congress provided financial support, albeit somewhat grudgingly.[1] A subsequent fair would give Mrs. Fairbanks opportunity for international as well as national recognition. Americans in 1904 sang "Meet Me in St. Louis," and millions of them did so at the Louisiana Purchase Exposition along with countless visitors from around the globe—several hundred thousand on any given day. There were fifty thousand exhibits from all over the world. Three hundred organizations held meetings there from May through November 1904.[2] The Board of Lady Managers for the St. Louis World's Fair was originally chaired by a woman of social prominence, Mrs. James Blair, whose husband was involved in planning the exposition. The Missouri Federation of Women's Clubs had proposed a woman with more experience in national women's clubs, but the male president of the Louisiana Purchase Exposition Company did not appoint her, thus losing the support of the Federation for the Board of Lady Managers. Although there were other women on the board who had organizational experience, they were unable to acquire sufficient funds and support for the work of the board. When Mrs. Blair's husband became involved in a financial scandal involving one of his legal clients, the Blairs left St. Louis and any connection to the fair.[3]

Mrs. Daniel Manning, former president general and now the first honorary president general of the DAR, was selected as the new chairman of the Board of Lady Managers for the Louisiana Purchase Exposition. She used her political connections in Washington to force Congress to provide the one hundred thousand dollars they had initially earmarked for the Board of Lady Managers. The women were able to furnish their rooms in the designated building, entertain dignitaries, and contribute to funding a nursery and facility for women open to the public at the Model City exhibition on the main fairgrounds.[4] The women's designated building had a reception room; reading, writing, and resting rooms for women; and a hospital room with a trained nurse who was under the supervision of the medical director of the fair. There was a room for the DAR and another for the Colonial Dames society.[5]

The long-standing rivalry between Mrs. Manning and Mrs. Donald McLean for preeminence in the DAR continued at the St. Louis Fair. Mrs. Fairbanks's four-year tenure as president general was coming to a close. It was generally accepted that Mrs. McLean would be elected to succeed her. However, Mrs. Manning, who had served only two years as president, wanted another two-year term and was planning to run again.

The DAR of Missouri with the DAR groups of all the other Louisiana Purchase states celebrated Flag Day, June 14, 1904, at the Missouri Building. Mrs. Donald McLean, Regent of the New York chapter, gave an address at the St. Louis celebration.[6] Mrs. McLean was the guest of the William H. Thompsons in St. Louis. Thompson, president of the National Bank of Commerce, was treasurer of the Louisiana Purchase Exposition Company, and his wife was on the Board of Lady Managers.

Given that Mrs. Manning was president of the Board of Lady Managers and wanted to run again for president general of the DAR, there was concern among some local members that Mrs. McLean, also in the running for the next DAR election, was coming to St. Louis as the guest of St. Louisans. It was feared "that her coming here might inject a little politics into World's Fair society," the *St. Louis Post-Dispatch* reported on June 17, 1904.

Mrs. Fairbanks did not attend the Flag Day celebration. She was busy elsewhere. Delegates were gathering in Chicago for the National Republican Convention that opened officially on June 21. Theodore Roosevelt was not in favor of Charles Fairbanks as a vice presidential candidate. Senator Fairbanks's public statements to the press indicated that he was not actively seeking the nomination, but Indiana associates suggested that he would accept if nominated.[7] Ultimately, both Roosevelt and Fairbanks were unanimously nominated by the convention.

On the evening of his nomination, Mr. and Mrs. Fairbanks held a reception in the lobby of their hotel. While politicians from around the country were congratulating him, the women took her to "the ladies' entrance" of the lobby to offer congratulations to her.[8] "Many women prominent in the life of Chicago" called on her and numerous congratulatory telegrams were sent by "prominent women identified with Mrs. Fairbanks in the work of the Daughters of the American Revolution." The following morning the DAR members in Chicago honored her at a reception at the Lincoln Club.[9] Mrs. Fairbanks told a reporter, "I am feeling most happy and have had an exceedingly pleasant time at the convention."[10] It hadn't been all behind-the-scenes political maneuvering. The Chicago *Inter Ocean* showed a half page of pictures of "Men and Women of National Fame Whose Faces Are Growing Familiar in Chicago," including one of Mrs. Fairbanks in an open touring car with a woman friend who was driving—both fashionably dressed, including large hats, as they left the hotel for a spin.[11]

Charles, Nellie, and their son Frederick, accompanied by Indiana and national politicians, made a whistle-stop train tour from Chicago through Indiana to Indianapolis.[12] In Indianapolis, they were met by thousands of local citizens who escorted them to their home where a ladies' committee had arranged a reception on the lawn. The vice presidential nominee was much moved, his voice tremulous as he rose to speak.[13]

Mrs. Fairbanks did attend the St. Louis fair later to great acclaim. Pictures of her appeared on the front pages of local papers accompanied by lengthy articles. At this World's Fair, the DAR was celebrating the fourteenth anniversary of its founding on October 11, 1890.[14] It was noted that there was no evidence of factions at this gathering, although there seemed to "a little undercurrent." There were "straws to suggest that while Mrs. Donald McLean was not present in person her spirit was not far away."[15]

Mrs. Fairbanks acted as peacemaker before this event. Members of the St. Louis chapter were upset by a remark that Mrs. Manning had made to the effect that the St. Louis Daughters had not done as much as they might have done in preparing DAR activities. They were threatening not to attend a luncheon to be given by Mrs. Manning in honor of Mrs. Fairbanks, excusing their behavior by saying that the event would be crowded and there would be little room for them. All of this was called to the attention of Mrs. Fairbanks, who said, "Of course the St. Louis Daughters will attend the luncheon. There is no reason for them to feel offended. They have certainly done everything that could be expected of them in preparing for the convention. If there isn't room for all at the luncheon, we'll find a way to make room."[16] The St. Louis Daughters attended the luncheon.

A woman reporter attended another luncheon for Mrs. Fairbanks, given at one of the dining rooms at the fair, by other prominent members of the DAR. They drank a toast to "Our President-General." Mrs. Fairbanks bowed, smiling, and replied, "To the right woman in the right place, my successor that is to be. May she be happy. May she be successful. May she do much good for Continental Hall. May she do right."[17] She was wishing the probable successor, Mrs. McLean, happiness and success, but perhaps warning that it would be right to continue the path to completion of Continental Hall.

A DAR member had told the reporter, "You will like Mrs. Fairbanks. She is the kind of woman other women love because of her sweetness of manner, her knowledge and consideration of others." The reporter thought that Mrs. Fairbanks could influence others by her smile alone, but wondered that "[i]t is not ... often that women whom other women love ... make the best presiding officers." She inquired of Mrs. Wallace Delafield, State Regent of Missouri, who was sitting next to her, how Mrs. Fairbanks could be beloved and yet an efficient presiding officer. Mrs. Delafield explained, "Mrs. Fairbanks is successful because she can control her feelings. Even when a vote is being taken, no one who watches her knows which side she wishes to win." The reporter asked Mrs. Fairbanks how she could do it and received the reply, "Just think that each woman is voting right—as she sees it. Then it's easy." Mrs. Fairbanks also commented that she thought politics to be "good fun."[18]

A group of prominent foreigners was sitting nearby in the same dining room. Prior to the toast and Mrs. Fairbanks's reply, the restaurant band had played the French national anthem, "La Marseillaise," and the gentlemen sang the words. The DAR women, ever cognizant of the role of France in the American Revolution, applauded. The band played the "Star Spangled Banner." The DAR ladies stood. Then the foreigners requested that the band play "America," and everyone in the restaurant stood and sang.[19]

The DAR anniversary celebration opened at 10:30 a.m. on Tuesday, October 11, 1904, with Mrs. Fairbanks presiding, after prolonged applause as she came to the platform. David R. Francis, former mayor of St. Louis and governor of Missouri and now the driving force behind the Louisiana Purchase Exposition, gave the welcoming address. Next, Missouri State Regent Delafield introduced Mrs. Fairbanks.[20]

Mrs. Fairbanks included in her speech a plea for acceptance into the DAR of the Daughters of the Revolution, a splinter group that had been formed in the 1890s by a disgruntled DAR member who felt that she had not been given sufficient recognition at the founding of the DAR.

President General Fairbanks proclaimed:

"It is in no minor key that I would speak to you today but in hopes of loud acclaim and genuine congratulations upon the matchless achievements attained during the years since last it was my pleasure to greet you.

"Do you wonder, my daughters, for such you will ever be to me, no matter from what section of this fair land you come; I say, do you wonder that my heart swells with just pride and that the tears are ready to start, as I gaze upon this great assembly of representative women, gathered from far and near to commemorate the natal day of our beloved society.

"Where was its beginning? Whence did it come? I know that time limits will not permit, yet we will take a rapid glance backward and review in brief the wondrous start, development and growth of the national society.

"The first wave of inspiration which swept from the Pacific coast to the Atlantic seaboard came from the Sons of the American Revolution and resulted in the rapid formation of many chapters of that organization.

"The daughters of revolutionary sires soon caught the infection. Indeed, the contagion had been long in the air, and it became apparent that if they were to accomplish any patriotic work, it must be within their own circle and under their own leadership. The ardor and zeal of a few undaunted women never flagged, and their determination to organize a distinctive daughters' society became a fixed purpose. In their efforts to place before the country the objects and aims of a daughters' association they were ably assisted by Col. W. H. McDowell, whose valiant efforts in their behalf and valuable services have always been fully appreciated by the daughters. Mrs. Mary S. Lockwood also gained eternal fame by arousing renewed interest in the heroism of women by her review of an old revolutionary story, "Hannah Arnett's Faith," which appeared in the *Washington Post,* July 13, 1890. "No one who has not felt the dispiriting heat of a summer morning in Washington can quite realize the heroism in calling any kind of a meeting in August in the almost forsaken capital. However, in spite of heat and the absence of many persons already interested in the movement, these brave women held their first meeting at the residence of Mrs. Louis Knowlton Brown on K Street about July 25."

Mrs. Fairbanks briefly outlined the history of the DAR, its aims, and its accomplishments, and went on to discuss current work:

"It hardly seems necessary to refer to the wondrous achievements of the few past years. The work accomplished during the Spanish-American War alone would have given deserved renown to the national society and placed it foremost in the rank of patriotic organizations. But time will not permit a further review.

"In the few moments left there is one thought, one long-cherished hope, very near my heart, which I would emphasize as, perhaps, the highest aspiration within the grasp of the national Society. I refer to the union of the Daughters of the Revolution and the Daughters of the American Revolution.

"If not mistaken, it was my privilege to have appointed the first committee of the Daughters of the American Revolution to confer with a similar committee of the Daughters of the Revolution. The coveted prize seemed just within our grasp.

"However, slight differences prevented a consolidation, and since then other committees have worked with the same end in view, but have met with a like result.

"In the report of the state regent of Colorado, she states that 'in January last a large number of the most active workers among the Daughters of the Revolution resigned and joined the Daughters of the American Revolution' and it was hoped by this action to bring about similar efforts in other sections of the country thus uniting together under one banner all Revolutionary Daughters.

"It does seem as if this effort might be the entering wedge and that the example of the Colorado daughters might open wide the door to happy union. You remember the old French proverb 'It is the first step that costs.' Are you ready to take that step?"

Mrs. Fairbanks had mitigated Mrs. Manning's abrasiveness, referred to the sexism of the majority of the Sons of the American Revolution with tact, given credit to the membership of the DAR— not to herself—for accomplishments of the organization, honored the founders of the organization, and shown her grasp of history. She demonstrated an understanding of leadership that would have served her well had she been able to enter national politics.

Chapter Eleven

BUILDING A STATELY MANSION

From the beginning of their organization in 1890, the Daughters of the American Revolution had wanted a building for national headquarters in Washington. Efforts in that direction had been made but had not come to fruition. When Mrs. Fairbanks became president general, things changed.

Mrs. Mary Lockwood, one of the four DAR founders, wrote, "Her administration was begun in the midst of the agitation of a great business enterprise to which the National Society had long been committed. This was the project of building a Memorial Continental Hall, which was causing lively discussion and rapidly assuming tangible form."[1] Former President General Mrs. Adlai Stevenson referred to the administration of Mrs. Fairbanks as the "constructive period."[2]

President General Fairbanks gave a report at the 1902 Continental Congress as chairman of the Memorial Hall Committee:

"Your Continental Hall committee has held nine different meetings during this year. The interest in Continental Hall has been very strong. The Board has been represented upon this committee by various chapter regents, and persons, members of the society, have been represented. The interest has been very general. In May, we met and during that meeting there were … committees formed … the chairmen of these various subcommittees have been very faithful and very zealous in their duties. We have given great thought to this subject [of a site]. We have desired an ideal place for your Continental Hall. We have felt that we were not building for this year or the next decade, not for the next generation, but perhaps for several generations to come.

"We have had great divisions among us [as to a site near the White House, on Capitol Hill, or in the residential area in the northwest section of the city]. But your committee has had to take into consideration the fact that our hall, while we desire and wish that it could never be used for anything but the uses of the Daughters of the American Revolution, should be a temple dedicated to the liberty, the loyalty, and the memory of the fathers and mothers of the Revolution. Yet we have found it necessary to take some sordid thought into consideration. We have found it was necessary that we should erect a hall in which there should be an assembly room that we could rent to other societies, an auditorium which conventions coming here would seek, which if accessible would bring in a large revenue. We look forward to the time when the Continental Hall will accommodate many such societies and conventions, and thus we will support our temple of liberty, our memorial to our fathers and mothers.

"For this reason we have deemed it wise that we should purchase a site in the central part of the city.

"At the last meeting of the Continental Hall committee it was resolved upon to seek a certain site, and it was passed. There was, I am bound to say, a large and respectable minority against the choice of the majority, and we were not enabled to make the purchase of this site because of the lack of three-fourths of the National Board of Management being present to permit us to carry our these instructions. So we have come to you tonight to help us upon this, to help to select a site. We could not have the Board of Management because they had not arrived."[3] Mrs. Fairbanks went directly to the membership, which seemed more likely to respond positively to her beautifully phrased and passionate pleas for Memorial Continental Hall than the committee. After lengthy discussion about all aspects of the building, the site was approved by the delegates. Nellie Fairbanks had been on the board of the Propylaeum in Indianapolis as it was planned and built for meetings and other activities of women's clubs there. Charles had been one of the lawyers who served as consultants, and she undoubtedly had participated both in her official role and in her usual cooperation in the work of her husband. From her work in Indianapolis, she recognized the necessity to take "some sordid thought into consideration." It would be very useful in supporting the Memorial Hall to be able to rent space to other appropriate organizations as the Propylaeum did in Indianapolis.

As a result of her experience, President General Fairbanks was well aware that enthusiasm and support from members would be necessary; money raised; land purchased; and architectural and legal consultation obtained. Her campaign covered the country—every state then in the Union, as well as territories not yet states—to encourage and compliment DAR groups in their local projects and to elicit support and donations for the projected Continental Memorial Hall. Back in the District of Columbia, she and her Memorial Continental Hall Committee set about obtaining land and constructing a building in spite of road blocks attempted by some—"of which there were not a few of the most formidable lions in the way," as Mary Lockwood put it. Mrs. Lockwood also noted, "Mrs. Fairbanks took hold ... and grappled with the finances in a masterly way, and, while the duties of the Building Committee have from the start been onerous, she always backed it up with a warmth that has kept their courage up, thus enabling them to overcome all obstacles ... It was at Mrs. Fairbanks home that the initial movements to purchase ground were consummated ... and the documents and deeds of transfer on the real-estate purchased were signed. In everything that pertained to this movement she has been an element of strength."[4]

The first meeting of the Memorial Continental Hall Committee at the Fairbanks home was on June 4, 1902, less than five months after she had first presided at the annual congress of the DAR. In the course of their meetings, Professor William R. Ware, of Columbia University, New York, was selected as an expert consultant, and General John M. Wilson and Mr. Bernard R. Green were invited to act as advisers for the committee.[5] At a later meeting, the National Board of Management of the DAR, acting on recommendations of the Memorial Continental Hall Committee, authorized the purchase of land at Seventeenth and D Streets, near Connecticut Avenue, in the District of Columbia for the building site "to have and to hold forever."[6] This location made possible the address, 1776 D Street, a number appropriate for a Revolutionary War memorial. Initially, the United States Congress had donated land for the site of the proposed memorial hall, but legal difficulties arose over that arrangement. "That did not halt Mrs. Fairbanks. She called her counselors together on frequent occasions. Each time she presented new solutions of the problem until finally success came and the society bought its own site in the heart of Washington."[7] Mrs. Fairbanks later reported on the details of negotiation, noting that the subcommittee on the site had investigated purchase of adjacent land, but that the owners had insisted on an exorbitant price. The subcommittee was of the opinion that the purchase they had made would fit current needs. The site had cost over $50,000, but contributions and funds previously set aside for the purpose had been generous enough to cover land purchase and to begin construction of the building itself.[8] Mrs.

Fairbanks presided over ground-breaking ceremonies on October 11, 1902:

"Today we are assembled at a point in our history which is of exceeding interest to the Daughters of the American Revolution.

"Twelve years ago today, exactly at this hour, were lain the great lines upon which our society is based; by a happy coincidence, we are here to commemorate their action. There are perhaps present but few of those who organized on that date, but today we stand as representatives of a great and patriotic society, the result of their work, which now has upon its lists over 40,000 members.

"This is a society not devoted to any ulterior or selfish purpose. We are here because we represent those virtues for which our forefathers struggled, achieved and oft times lost life and fortune in building up. We are not here in any pride of family or blood. We are here to aid in preserving the eternal principles of liberty, and it behooves us not to think of the society alone, it behooves us to think greatly of the splendid work achieved by our revered ancestors, the men and women of the Revolution, and to do our humble best to emulate that work and aid in preserving intact the splendid heritage of free homes, a free country where prevail the principles of justice and liberty.

"We have reached a great point in the history of our organization, for today we will break the ground—we will turn over the first spade full of earth upon which, in the near future, shall be builded the massive foundations of our beautiful Memorial Continental Hall, which shall be resplendent in the beauty of lettering of gold, artistic carving, stately columns as tributes to the love and patriotism of the great army of the Revolution, the men of the line, and that grandest of reserve corps, the women of the Revolution, who held the fortress of the home, who raised the flax, who spun the wool, and wove the cloth and cut and made the garments of the heroes, who fought so bravely and so well the battles of liberty and progress.

"So now, we, the Daughters of their lineage, proud to be called the Daughters of their immortal struggle for independence, and for the possession of those sacred, inalienable rights of humanity 'life, liberty, and the pursuit of happiness;' we gladly come to this historic spot, to first break ground for the erection of our Temple of Liberty.

"As the Greeks thought it their bounden duty to build for the victors of Salamis and Thermopylae testimonials of remembrance of their thrilling deeds of valor, let us take joy in the thought that in the building of this modern Parthenon, we render tribute to battles fought not for dominion, but fought in the holy cause of freedom.

"In this sacred duty, it was hoped that all the surviving founders of our glorious society, might have participated … But we are sorry to say that Mrs. Ellen Hardin Walworth deeply regrets her inability to be present, and I also grieve to announce the serious illness of Miss Mary Desha … One week since, in the midst of her labors upon the ways and means committee for Memorial Continental Hall, she was stricken down by a well-nigh fatal illness.

"Another one of our founders who bore the illustrious name dear to all Americans, that of [Eugenia] Washington, has been summoned to her rest, ere these strong steps toward building Memorial Continental Hall had been taken. But we have the inspiring presence of her whom we all delight to see, upon whose judgment and counsel we may safely rely, she whose gifted pen, so powerfully told the thrilling story … [that] served as the bugle call to marshal the mighty hosts of the Daughters of the American Revolution. I have the honor and pleasure of introducing Mrs. Mary S. Lockwood."[9]

It was raining during the ground-breaking ceremonies, but the weather didn't deter Mrs. Fairbanks and Mrs. Lockwood from stepping out from the ceremonial tent. Mrs. Lockwood, breaking ground, "used a copper spade, presented by the Montana Chapter of the Daughters of the American Revolution. The blade is of copper from Montana mines, and the handle is of wood cut from the path the Virginians, Lewis and Clark, trod when they first explored [the west] ... It was decorated with ribbons given by the Mary Washington Colonial Chapter, of New York All sections of this vast land were thus recognized in this symbolic spade."[10] Mrs. Lockwood planted Osage orange seeds in flower pots for each of the original states as well as additional ones in another container for states later admitted to the union. These were cared for in the gardens of the United States Department of Agriculture until the next national Continental Congress of the DAR in spring 1903 when the young "Liberty Trees" were presented to State Regents to plant in their home states to symbolize the spirit of American Independence and the growth of the women's patriotic society.[11]

A block of white marble from the White House was to be used in the interior of the building. This marble was inscribed "From the home of the First President General of the Daughters of the American Revolution" (Carolyn Scott Harrison, wife of President Benjamin Harrison). On February 23, 1903, the Sons of the American Revolution of the District of Columbia gave a "handsome flag, which was planted on the site where the ground was broken. This flag floating over this ground secures the legal right of the Society to this property, as authorized by the District [of Columbia] Commissioners."[12]

At the annual meeting sessions after she was unanimously elected to her second term as president general in 1903, Mrs. Fairbanks reported as chairman of the Continental Memorial Hall committee that plans were progressing, and funds for the work were growing. Inspiring the Daughters to continue contributions to this memorial to the Father of the Country, she pointed out that the location of the purchased land is "under the shadow not only of the national home of the nation's president, but of that towering and impressive obelisk that is honored with the name of Washington" [the White House and the Washington Monument]. After she concluded, "We may have been liberal in the past, but in the future let us be as liberal ten times over," the acting chairman had difficulty bringing order to an outburst of applause from all the gathered delegates.[13]

The chairman of the Congressional committee was able to report that a bill exempting the ground from taxation had been passed by both the United States Senate and the House of Representatives.[14] No doubt of assistance, Senator Fairbanks of Indiana chaired the Senate Committee on Public Buildings and Grounds of the capital.

The Continental Memorial Hall committee presented Mrs. Fairbanks with a silver loving cup in honor of her work as chairman, "your personal efforts, your untiring activity, and your wise counsel … your hand has guided and your brain has devised the methods of work, and your heart has inspired us all with its own warm enthusiasm." Mrs. Fairbanks replied, "Ladies and co-workers, I need not tell you how touched I am by this beautiful token of your regard and esteem, nor can I thank you enough. It is, indeed, far beyond my deserts, but not less loving nor less beautiful than your friendship which has inspired it. I accept it, and I thank you."[15] Resuming the chair after the presentation, she declared that she was in a "very receptive frame of mind" and asked the delegates to bring forth the contributions raised by each state chapter during the year. Over $50,000 was brought forward, individual gifts of members ranging from $1 to $2,000.[16] Later that evening, delegates viewed stereopticon pictures of the eight building plans being considered. A competition for plans for the building, open to all American architects, had been held. Seventy plans were originally submitted. Ultimately, the plans of architect Edward P. Casey were selected. Only American materials were used in the marble building. On the south side were thirteen columns in a colonnade to honor the original states.[17]

On April 19, 1904, Mrs. Fairbanks presided over stirring ceremonies, conducted by the Masonic Order, to lay the cornerstone of the new building. Lighted candles graced each corner of the stone during the impressive rites.[18] President General Fairbanks used the same gavel that George Washington had used in similar ceremonies at the National Capitol in 1793.[19] The invocation was led by the Rev. Edward Everett Hale, Chaplain of the United States Senate. The Children of the American Revolution gave the salute to the flag, and music was provided by the Marine Band. Greetings were received "from far and wide." Mrs. Fairbanks delivered an address "so eloquent that it stirred the great audience to enthusiasm."[20]

She said, "The spacious marble hall ... is an expression from this great society of its broad and comprehensive view of those characters in the past to whom gratitude is due. It is not erected alone to the mighty statesmen of the revolutionary epoch ... not alone to the immortal generals who organized the patriots into armies ... not alone to the heroic captains of the infant navy ... not alone to the inspiring sacrifices of a Rebecca Mott, who so loved the cause of liberty that she burned her own house ... not alone [to] brave Molly Pitcher to carry out the work which sudden death took from her husband, but to all the men of the line and all the women at the spinning wheel."[21]

Later that year, she was able to report that construction workers had laid the foundations.[22] She wrote to regents of the chapters around the country, "The work on Continental Hall goes bravely forward. A solid foundation is being laid where soon shall rise the walls of our memorial. The work is being thoroughly done under the best of supervision." She also suggested that if each member would contribute five dollars, sufficient funds would be available.[23] At the time, such a sum would more than cover the price of a nice hotel room for one day as indicated in information in the same publication for members who wanted to visit the Louisiana Exposition in St. Louis.

The work of construction progressed rapidly. The *Washington Evening Star* commented, "It is the costliest and most impressive monument of its kind ever built by women in this country or any other … the first building dedicated to all the recognized heroes of the American Revolution: men and women alike. From the artistic standpoint, it is one of the finest buildings which the beautiful capital contains, and from the utilitarian it is destined to become one of the most useful."[24]

Chapter Twelve

MEMORIAL TO THE PAST, INCENTIVE FOR THE FUTURE

Memorial Continental Hall was dedicated at an impressive ceremony on April 17, 1905. Addresses were delivered by Senator Dolliver of Iowa and French Ambassador Jusserand. The ambassador announced that a bas relief of the Founding Fathers of America from the base of a famous French statue would be given for the Memorial Hall. The Marine Band played courtesy of the United States government. Clergymen from several denominations were present. Mrs. Fairbanks welcomed guests "to the dedication of Memorial Continental Hall, our Society's greatest enterprise, the symbol of its work and spirit whose doorstead we have faith to believe is:

'The Lintel low enough

To keep out pomp and pride,

The Threshold high enough

To turn deceit aside.

The Doorband strong enough

From Robbers to defend.

This Door will open at a touch

To welcome every Friend.'"

She continued, "I dreamed that stone by stone was reared a sacred fane. A temple neither pagoda, mosque nor church, but loftier, ampler, always open doored to every breath from Heaven, and truth and peace and love and justice came and dwelt therein."[1]

"This dedication marks the realization of a resolution passed at the first meeting of our Society, October 1890, 'to erect a fireproof museum for revolutionary relics, possessions, and records of the Society.' Through varying fortunes and passing years, that plan has grown stronger, and with its growth becomes broader and more glorious its ideals, so that to the 'fireproof' museum has been added the archives, the offices, the auditorium, and finally, last and most beautiful, this memorial feature. The fact that a Society of women erects the structure makes it unique. Its memorial feature renders it sacred and great.

"It is a tribute of gratitude to the wise promoters of the War for Independence, to the heroic men who on land and sea achieved its triumph, to those generous-hearted allies from foreign lands, whose services may not be forgotten; to those loyal earnest women, the mothers of the Revolution ... [who] held the fortress of the home as a haven to which might return those who fought the battles which made of the struggling Colonies a vast Republic.

"This Memorial Continental Hall, which we dedicate today, is an acknowledgment which America owes to those who planned the mighty Revolution, those who managed its campaigns, conquered its foes, founded the greatest nation on earth, and formulated the beneficent laws for its government. Their sufferings, their devotion, not for their time alone, but for the long future, deserves and now has received, the hearty, unreserved recognition of those who are glad to name themselves Daughters of the American Revolution.

"This memorial building, only partially completed, is also designed for the headquarters for the society ... where will be held the Congresses of our Society ... which shall gather the Daughters from the North, the South, the East, and the West, even from the Islands of the sea, where each shall find a greeting, a welcome home...

"It is truly a memorial to patriots; it is also an incentive to all who behold it to keep ever living and active the principles of justice and liberty upon which it was founded. It is the mute, yet eloquent, protest against forgetfulness of American ideals, of American justice, and American humanity. It also the physical expression of the belief of the society, whose possessions and pride it is, for it brings to mind the lessons of patriotism, the perpetuation of liberty which that society was founded to promulgate, whose existence arose from devotion to country and from the fear that the addition to our country's population of subjects of despotic monarchies [who] were so imbued with hatred for government that they might endeavor to substitute anarchy for law and order, and thus compass the fall of the most humane and liberal institution of government ever known—those of republican America.

"From these fears sprang the Society of the Daughters of the American Revolution, which with kindred patriotic organizations, is reawakening the love for liberty and is teaching its principles. It believes that its aims are to be attained best by diffusion of knowledge concerning the men and women of the Revolutionary period, their beliefs, and their patriotic work. These are taught by Daughters of the American Revolution in the great cities of our country to the children of foreign parentage, as well as to those who are 'to the manner born.' Study of Revolutionary history is everywhere encouraged. It is believed that tablets and monuments erected to immortalize the lovers of freedom serve as reminders, as admonition to all who behold them.

"This society having erected all over the land tablets and monuments, has at last reared this token of its veneration and gratitude to those who made this country free and great. Reared it not only for the statesmen and leaders, but to the men who carried the muskets in the ranks, to the women at the spinning wheel...

"[T]his day, April 17, 1905, a date significant ... for now the representatives of fifty thousand members of this society assembled in Continental Congress, for the first time in their own auditorium with their own roof above them, their own walls surrounding them, their own ground beneath their feet. The dream has 'come true.'"[2] Mrs. Fairbanks was bringing together in one address all that she believed the Memorial Continental Hall to symbolize: the sacrifices of the men in the trenches and the women at the spinning wheel who had won American freedom and the current projects of the society to educate children as well as adults—not only those of foreign parentage but also those of long-established American families—about the founding of the United States on the "principles of justice and liberty."

The founding of the Society—in part based on the fear that people who had experienced despotism would be disposed to violence against any government— occurred at a time when there were many immigrants to both coasts of the country. Harsh laws had been aimed at Asian immigrants on the west coast. There was unfair treatment of immigrants to the east coast from southern and eastern Europe. The occasional immigrant who promoted anarchy or other extreme views was seen by some as prototypical of all recent immigrants—immigrants who were not Anglo-Saxon and Protestant. The feeling was enhanced by reaction to the recent assassination of President McKinley by a man of immigrant parentage—as powerful emotionally for Americans of the time as reactions to the later assassination of President Kennedy or of the near assassination of President Reagan.

"Nativist and racist violence erupted over immigration. Anti-immigrant forces organized their hatred into powerful institutions like the Immigrant Restriction League and the Ku Klux Klan."[3] Less severe tactics employed by the public schools included giving all instruction in English, making civics a required course, instituting home room meetings as a time of group guidance, and expanding extracurricular activities like student government and athletics to promote unity and cooperation.[4]

In a speech to the Senate, Charles Fairbanks had mentioned important contributions of immigrants to the country. Native and foreign-born in Indiana had "been zealous co-workers, sharing alike in all the labors, anxieties, and rewards incident to carving out of the wilderness that majestic commonwealth." Until recently, homestead laws and other measures had favored immigrants. However, they had come primarily from the United Kingdom, Germany, and the Scandinavian countries. More recent immigrants did not seem as interested in home and family and often included "the most ignorant pauper laborers from abroad." He emphasized education, concluding that his proposals were born neither of "a want of hospitality nor of a nativistic spirit, but of profound conviction that illiterate elements do not make for national betterment." Only those who can "read and write our Constitution and are enamored of our country and its institutions" should be admitted.[5] Nellie Fairbanks, perhaps with a more benevolent view, promoted education of all children about positive aspects of patriotism, including teaching the foreign born in the languages of their nations of origin. Education helped immigrants to meet citizenship requirements and to begin their search for the American Dream. Complex questions about immigration remain with us today, including concerns about those who do not speak English.

In her last welcoming address to the DAR as president general in 1905, after the dedication of the Memorial Hall, Mrs. Fairbanks said:

"We have reached a height from which we may review the small beginnings, the increasing members, the grand work, and the beneficent purposes exercised by this society. Let us continue to labor with undiminished effort and unremitting zeal to emphasize this example of liberty. I wish it were possible for every Daughter ... to visit the headquarters and investigate the work accomplished there. I feel that they would carry back to their homes information which would surely make more clear to the various chapters the work which is being carried out at the national center. All of the departments are increasing in size, and consequently in work.

"My welcome to you today must also be my farewell. For over four years I have gone in and out among you bearing the honors and responsibilities of the position which you conferred upon me. I may truly say to you that I have been devoted to the great purposes which have come under my control, that in whatever I have done, I have been solicitous of the welfare and advancement of our society. I shall at the end of this week relinquish the commission with which you have endowed me. I have during these years formed friendships which shall ever be most dear to me; I have formed associations which my retirement from the leadership of this of this devoted organization shall not break. With a heart full of gratitude, I assure you of my love and appreciation of all the kindness and of all the aid, all the counsel which you have rendered me, and I bespeak for my successor [Mrs. Donald McLean] the same generous support. I wish to express the hope that your counsels together will be marked with harmony; that you may go from here with renewed resolution to carry on to success the great efforts of our society."

She then asked representative regents from the North, the West, the South, and the East to bring good tidings from each of their "sections of this great republic."[6]

In a later letter to Mrs. Stevenson, Mrs. Fairbanks wrote, "I appreciate highly what you were pleased to say of the work, which I had the joy to be able to assist in performing while President General. I shall not soon forget, indeed I never shall forget, the steadfast, whole hearted, enthusiastic support of the devoted 'Daughters' who came at my call, to decide upon the purchase of the site for our building … The events of my term were possessed of the deepest interest and many of them of greatest importance to the welfare of our Society. In answer to your inquiry as to that work which I consider of the greatest importance during my term, I will unhesitatingly say that the selection and purchase of our admirable site, the breaking of the ground, the laying of the corner stone, the building and dedication of Memorial Continental Hall in the presence of distinguished guests and during the session of the Congress of the NSDAR must stand pre-eminent."[7]

The nation and its capital had seen a woman campaign across the country, raise considerable sums of money, complete projects of national importance including a unique building, and skillfully manage the components of a major national organization both publicly and behind the scenes. She had emphasized the roles of women in the history of the United States. A decade and a half later, women would begin to vote in national elections in America. Then would begin the gradual advance of women—not yet completed a century later—toward direct access to the corridors of power.

West Union School where Nellie Cole completed her education at public school. Her father was on the first school board of Union County, Ohio. Union County Ohio Historical Society

Judge Philander B. Cole, Marysville, Union County, Ohio 1815 – 1892, father and mentor of Cornelia Cole Fairbanks. Union County Ohio Historical Society

*Yearbook picture, Cornelia Cole, Ohio Wesleyan Female Seminary,
1872. Ohio Wesleyan University Historical Collection*

Monnett Hall, Ohio Wesleyan Female College: Cornelia Cole was graduated from college here in 1872. The female college became part of its brother institution, Ohio Wesleyan University, five years later. Ohio Wesleyan University Historical Collection

Union County Courthouse, Marysville, Ohio. Judge Cole practiced here in his later years. David Ficko photo.

*Union Block, Marysville, Ohio. Judge Cole's last
law office was on the second floor. David Ficko photo.*

*Group of friends and family pictured in front of the Cole home Marysville,
Ohio, circa 1904. Nellie Fairbanks is in next to last row, midway,
wearing large white hat. Union County Ohio Historical Society*

*Cole Family Gravestone, Oakdale Cemetery, Marysville, Ohio.
Cornelia Cole Fairbanks's parents, two brothers, and one sister
are buried here. The small metal star indicates her brother
Ulysses Cole's Civil War service. Author's photo.*

Oil portrait of Cornelia Cole Fairbanks as a young matron in Indianapolis.
Courtesy Fairbanks Hospital, Indianapolis, Indiana. David Ficko photo.

Original Propylaeum Building. In 1888-9, Nellie Fairbanks served on the board of women who planned this notable expression of the late nineteenth century women's movement. Bass Photo Co Collection, INDIANA HISTORICAL SOCIETY

Cornelia Cole Fairbanks, circa 1900. Union County Ohio Historical Society

*Mrs. Fairbanks delivers a speech at Jamestown,
VA, 1905. Photo courtesy NSDAR*

*Mrs. Fairbanks and distinguished guests at the dedication of
Memorial Continental Hall, 1905. Photo courtesy NSDAR*

Memorial Continental Hall today. Courtesy NSDAR. Mark Gulezian photo.

The Fairbanks's Indianapolis Home during the final year of Mrs. Fairbanks' life, the last building she planned. It now houses offices. David Ficko photo.

Nellie Fairbanks' grave, Crown Hill Cemetery, Indianapolis.
The commemorative marker was placed by the Cornelia Cole Fairbanks
Chapter, NSDAR, 2007, on the one hundredth anniversary
of the chapter's founding. David Ficko photo.

Fairbanks Monument, Crown Hill Cemetery, Indianapolis. David Ficko photo.

The face of the monument reads:

CHARLES WARREN FAIRBANKS
U. S. SENATE   1897 — 1905
VICE PRESIDENT THE
UNITED STATES   1905 — 1909

———————

CORNELIA COLE FAIRBANKS
PRESIDENT GENERAL
D. A. R.
1901 — 1905

Chapter Thirteen

WIFE OF THE VICE PRESIDENT

The metamorphosis of Charles Warren Fairbanks from a senator to the presiding officer of the United States Senate took less than two minutes. He had been a senator for eight years and would be vice president for four more. That morning, March 5, 1905, he had arisen at seven, dressed as usual, and breakfasted with his wife, his daughter, his eldest son and daughter-in-law, and a house guest.[1] The senate chamber where the oath of office was administered to him later that morning was filled with officials of the United States Government, the Washington diplomatic corps, and their families. Mrs. Fairbanks, their daughter and four sons, and his mother were among those present. The life journey of Fairbanks's mother was classic Americana. Her family left Connecticut via Conestoga wagon for Pittsburgh when she was a child, went by boat along the Ohio and Muskingum Rivers to eastern Ohio, and traveled by wagon to Union County. There she would later meet and marry Loriston Fairbanks.[2] Now their eldest son would be the second highest official in the country. Once Vice President Fairbanks took the gavel from the president pro tem of the Senate who had administered the oath, the country had a vice president for the first time since the assassination of his mentor President McKinley in 1901.

The inauguration of President Roosevelt would soon take place outside the Capitol on the balconies overlooking the grounds where the public gathered.

The new presiding officer addressed his once and future colleagues: "Senators: I enter upon the discharge of the duties of the position to which I have been called by my countrymen with grateful appreciation of the high honor and with a deep sense of its responsibilities. I have enjoyed the privilege of serving with you here for eight years... We submit what we have done to the impartial judgment of history. I can never forget the pleasant relations which have been formed during my service upon the floor of the Senate... They warrant the belief that I shall have, in the discharge of the functions which devolve upon me under the Constitution, the generous assistance and kindly forbearance of both sides of the chamber. We witness the majestic spectacle of a peaceful and orderly beginning of an administration of national affairs under the laws of a free and self-governing people. We pray that divine favor may attend it and that peace and progress, justice and honor may abide with our country and our countrymen."[3] The Republican ticket elected in November 1904 was balanced by candidates who were in almost every way opposites—President Theodore Roosevelt and Vice President Charles Warren Fairbanks: one from an old, established eastern family, the other from a family that had come to America at about the same time but had continued to push westward with the frontier; one a progressive whose views were heralding the new vision of the twentieth century, the other who represented the end of an era of conservative Republican politics in the nineteenth century; one ebullient, if not manic, the other whose dignified reserve in public had earned him an epithet, "the icicle."[4] It was sometimes facetiously remarked that the new vice president owed half his success to his wife—her gracious temperament, her cordial handshake and genial greeting, that had led to her great popularity.[5] Now well known as retiring president general of the DAR and an outstanding hostess in the nation's capital, Nellie Fairbanks would continue to be her husband's comrade and advisor. As a hostess, she had "proved to be a valuable asset to her husband."[6] At the Inaugural Ball that night, Mrs. Fairbanks "looked splendid in a gown of heavy white satin woven with big gold roses in a design alternating with smaller single roses of white, the whole beauty of the gown lying in the full sweeping train and the plain clinging effect of the front of the skirt... her hair in a simple fashion, coiled high on her head [with] a becoming ornament of tips and jewels ... a necklace and pendant of diamonds."[7] The next day, Vice President and Mrs. Fairbanks gave a reception at their home for about seventy guests—members of their family and alumni of Ohio Wesleyan University, including the current governor of Ohio and an Ohio Congressman. Among those faculty in attendance was a woman, Professor Clara Nelson. The school had come a long way since the days of Nellie Cole at Ohio Wesleyan Female College. Alumni living in the Washington area presented the new vice president and his wife with a collection of appealing scenes of Delaware, Ohio, drawn by a graduate of the school.[8]

Addressing large gatherings and conferences and talking to reporters would become frequent activities for Charles Fairbanks. He opened the International Railway Congress in Washington remarking on the public duty of railroads and advocating public and fixed rates with "just regard to the owners, the employees, and the public,"[9] discussed the commercial and social development of the country before a chamber of commerce in Pennsylvania decrying the segregation of the poor in urban areas and speaking for attention to the welfare of all members of communities,[10] and gave his views on labor unions to a California reporter, suggesting that "the organization of labor and capital go hand in hand," and labor organizations "must be free with all the prerogatives which pertain to freedom."[11] He was granted LL.D. degrees by the University of Iowa[12] and Northwestern University,[13] delivering commencement addresses at both institutions. Mrs. Fairbanks loved to travel and likely accompanied him when she was able and no doubt still offered constructive comment on his speeches. She continued busily in her work in national organizations. Unfortunately, in the winter season of 1906–07, Nellie was suffering from illness and exhaustion and spent time at health resorts regaining her strength. Mrs. Timmons, the Fairbanks's daughter, was able to serve as her father's hostess for Washington social affairs.

Initially, it had appeared that Theodore Roosevelt's plea (when he was vice president) that the vice president be given a larger role in government[14] would indeed come to fruition when he was president. In June 1905, less than four months into the administration, *Leslie's Weekly* reported that when President Roosevelt had started on his vacation that summer he had asked Fairbanks to represent him at the Lewis and Clark centennial ceremonies in Portland, Oregon, and at the International Railway Convention in Washington, D.C.[15]

In addition, "At Roosevelt's request Fairbanks, at a formal function at the White House, near the close of [the Railway Convention] received its members and did them the honors just as if he himself was at the head of the nation. No such distinction as this was ever before conferred on the second officer of the government by the first officer." The *Weekly* went on to comment optimistically, "Here is an era of good feeling between President and Vice President which sets an example that all future heads of the nation should follow."[16] There were just too many differences for this apparent rapprochement to last. Vice presidential historian Mark O. Hatfield, a former senator himself, suggested that although Fairbanks felt comfortable with his old friends in the Senate and enjoyed presiding there, in fact Roosevelt gave him little else to do. Fairbanks and the Republicans were "able to play a role in passing the president's ambitious legislative program that included the Hepburn Act regulating railroad rates, the Pure Food and Drug Act, and an employer's liability law for the District of Columbia." In the last half of the administration, 1907–08, Roosevelt fought with Congress over legislation that would add to the power of the executive. Fairbanks's sympathies lay with the Senate.[17]

Then, as now, views of nominally conservative or progressive politicians were not as simple to distinguish as it might seem. Biographer Kevin Phillips portrayed conservative McKinley as being more like his progressive successor Roosevelt than is generally assumed. He exhibited "greater acceptance of labor unions and railroad regulation than prevailed among Eastern conservatives, support for civil service reform, and opposition to the national party influence and patronage demands ... periodic willingness to compromise money issues of gold versus silver ... and represented a commitment to the people and their rule, the 'touch of Lincoln' that Midwest Republicans of that era thought so effective."[18] Fairbanks, a younger friend of McKinley, was a Midwest Republican and admirer of Lincoln. There were some issues about which the charismatic Roosevelt and his outwardly cold vice president held similar views—peacemaking, international trade, and conservation of natural resources. In 1905, Roosevelt was in the process of working out a settlement of the Russo-Japanese War, an endeavor for which he would win the Nobel Peace Prize. Fairbanks spoke at a banquet at the Waldorf-Astoria in New York in March 1905 about America's "high conception of right and justice among the nations of the earth" and appealed for arbitration of differences among nations,[19] and at a Fourth of July address in Ohio, praised the president's pointing "the way to the re-establishment of peace in the Orient."[20] At dedication exercises for the opening of the St. Mary's ship canal connecting Lake

Superior with the lower Great Lakes, Fairbanks praised the commerce between Canada and the United States, pointing out that there were no fortifications between the two countries and no battleships on the lakes.[21] Roosevelt, in complicated and controversial international dealings, was completing acquisition of the Panama Canal Zone.[22] The opening of the canal in 1914 would have an enormous impact on commerce among all nations.

Roosevelt had long been known as an avid outdoorsman and conservationist. A message from him, emphasizing the importance of keeping public forests in public hands, was read at the National Irrigation Conference in Boise in 1906. Vice President Fairbanks spoke at that same conference about the importance of irrigation in maintaining American farms and homes. Presciently he noted that farming was becoming a science and "the most successful farmer is the one who understands the chemistry of the soil and the products for which it is best suited."[23] He later founded the Indiana Forestry Association.[24]

Family matters were never far away in the life of the vice president and his wife. Their second son, Frederick, after graduating from Princeton, attended law school in Washington and worked for his senator father. When his father was vice president, Frederick worked for a manufacturing company run by an uncle in Springfield, Ohio.[25] At a party in Indianapolis in 1905, he was introduced to Helen Scott, the daughter of a Pittsburgh steel magnate. She was visiting one of her young woman friends in Indianapolis. A courtship began with visits back and forth. They became engaged but did not want an elaborate wedding. When they eloped to Steubenville, Ohio, in October 1906, each of the newlyweds sent a one sentence-telegram to his or her parents stating that they had been married—a "complete surprise to intimate friends and relatives."[26] On his way to make a speech in Iowa the next day, the vice president was greeted by reporters and said mischievously that he couldn't imagine why they wanted to interview him. When they mentioned his son's surprise marriage, he said playfully, "I can't discuss these social affairs."[27] An eager sheriff in Ohio later brought charges against Frederick because he, or a friend, had stated falsely that he was a resident of the county in which the marriage license was obtained. Local residents regretted the incident, attributing it to Frederick's being the son of a prominent father. His uncle and an attorney settled the legal matters.[28]

A year later, Charles and Nellie attended the Pittsburgh sesquicentennial celebration where the vice president gave an address, Mrs. Fairbanks was honored at a large reception, and they attended the christening of Fred and Helen's baby, Cornelia.[29]

Many areas of Vice President Fairbanks's interests occupied his time. In September 1905, he was among the dignitaries at a planning meeting in New York for the Inter-Church Conference on Federation to be held at Carnegie Hall in November of that year. An effort at Protestant ecumenism, it was the first "to which delegates have been named officially by the various Protestant denominations, previous conferences on missions and other topics having been unofficial in character."[30]

Although active in the Methodist Church all his life, Charles Fairbanks found that even such seemingly benign activity for a turn-of-the-century conservative Republican did not escape political uproar. Abstinence from alcohol use—temperance—at that time was comparable to abortion now as a highly controversial issue. Charles Fairbanks, like his mother before him, was a strong advocate of temperance.[31] On Memorial Day, 1907, President Roosevelt came to Indianapolis to dedicate the statue of an Indiana general. At a luncheon before the dedication, Vice President and Mrs. Fairbanks entertained about forty guests, described by Hoosier historian Ray Boomhower as a "veritable who's who of Indiana politics and literature." Unknown to the abstinent vice president, some of his Indianapolis friends felt it appropriate to serve cocktails to the president.[32] The vice president did not imbibe, but antiliquor newspapers around the country picked up the story of "Buttermilk Charlie" Fairbanks serving liquor at his table. He became "Cocktail Charlie." The story had broken in the *Indianapolis News* of which Fairbanks was a silent partner. Rumor had it that uproar ensued at the *News* after publication of the story because of fallout for Fairbanks's campaign for the 1908 Republican presidential nomination. Some later thought that the incident contributed to his defeat.[33] On the other hand, "If he lost votes among the Prohibitionists and the Methodists, it is likely that he gained as many votes among the German-Americans who passed resolutions strongly condemning the Methodist Conference and urging that the nation rally to the defense of the maligned Vice President."[34] Roosevelt's support of William Howard Taft for the nomination likely trumped temperance as a factor.

There is no question that the serving of alcoholic beverages on this occasion caused Fairbanks to lose another election—as delegate from Indiana to the Methodist Episcopal General Conference in Baltimore in 1908. Credit for his defeat was given to women attending the Indiana Conference electing national delegates. Many of them were members of the Women's Christian Temperance Union. They visited delegates and got their pledges to vote for Fairbanks's opponent.[35]

A Chicago Presbyterian publication investigated the incident. According to that report, a close friend of Mrs. Fairbanks made one last check of the luncheon table while Vice President and Mrs. Fairbanks were busy greeting their guests. Seeing no "drinkables" on the table, she ordered drinks from a fashionable private club. They were served at each place at the table, unbeknownst to the vice president until he came into the dining room. The Presbyterian paper opined that Methodists would soon regret "having inflicted so disproportionate a humiliation for a merely rumored charge of which the Vice President could have speedily cleared himself if he had been less a gentleman and readier to tell tales about the officiousness of his lady neighbor."[36] Roosevelt later told a Methodist Indiana Congressman, "I drank a cocktail out at Vice-President Fairbanks's home, whereupon all the members of your church landed on that gentleman and almost rode him out of the organization. That treatment was so uncalled for that, if it were not altogether ludicrous and preposterous, I would say it was simply outrageous." Furthermore, he added, "I don't like cocktails anyhow. I like champagne."[37]

In spite of the vice president's famous abstinence, it seems unlikely that such well-known hosts in Washington as the Fairbankses did not serve alcohol to their guests. When the Indianapolis incident first broke in the newspapers, Fairbanks wrote to a Methodist Bishop, "I followed the usual custom in such entertainments. For what was done, I was entirely responsible. I have never had any apologies to make for it." The Indianapolis caterer told a newspaper reporter, "Mrs. Fairbanks and her butler were to provide the wines and we were to serve them."[38] Mrs. Fairbanks was not quoted in accounts of the incident. She was accustomed to controversy—and to working behind the scenes.

Another area of controversy, then as now, was the impact of wealth on politics. The Gilded Age had ended, and the Progressive Age was in full swing. Charles Warren Fairbanks was very much a product of the Gilded Age. During the 1870s, he used inside information furnished by his uncles to amass a fortune of several million dollars. He became the western liaison for New York investment banker Austin Corbin, who advised him about investments. Although Fairbanks's methods would be objectionable today, they were legitimate at the time. Biographer

Herbert J. Rissler noted, "The acquisition of money never caused him to sacrifice his high moral code. His dealings were always legal and quite acceptable to the society in which he lived"—an age of "virtually unregulated capitalistic enterprise."[39]

He was accused of having used his money for a corrupt bargain to become a senator. He did spend his money liberally in the interests of the Republican Party and its candidates, but there was "no reason to believe that such a blatant 'deal' was ever consummated. Unfortunately, Fairbanks's supporters did include many whose primary interests lay in how their wealthy candidate might help in their own economic betterment."[40]

Muckraking articles in national magazines described the vice president unfavorably. *Cosmopolitan* "alleged ties between Fairbanks and J. P. Morgan, the nation's powerful banker, and railroad baron, E. H. Harriman." *Collier's Weekly* published articles for which the major source was a man who had been a secretary for Fairbanks in Washington. Fairbanks was portrayed as a financial speculator in bankrupt railroads who had treated workers unfairly while breaking railroad strikes and who had used his wealth to buy the vice presidential nomination. Fairbanks stated that the article was untrue, based on the word of a disgruntled former employee. Some of the so-called facts were not true and the "hyperbolic conclusions about sinister conduct" were false.[41] Fairbanks's biographer Rissler concluded that the charges in *Collier's Weekly* were "largely unsubstantiated" and that they were "one of the last gasps in the demise of the muckraking movement," adding that the "reason for the concentration upon the Vice President remains something of a mystery."[42]

There was a happier incident in the summer of 1907. While vacationing in Wisconsin with his family, Charles Fairbanks saw a young woman about to drown, rushed to the lake, and saved her life.

Characteristic of politics and the media, then and now, there were conflicting reports in the press as to just what his role had been—had he really been the one who saved her? However, even *Collier's Weekly*, no friend of Fairbanks, concluded that he had dived into thirty feet of water to save the young woman. It was a "public relations dream."[43]

Fairbanks continued his efforts to build up the Republican Party throughout the country, importantly in the South where both parties were competing for Negro votes. After a tremendous ovation, he addressed North Carolina Republicans at Greensboro: "Republican Government was ordained to promote justice, to secure each and all in the fullest possible enjoyment of equal rights and privileges under the law. Every American must stand before the law upon a plane of perfect equality with his fellow Americans."[44]

Fairbanks had his eye on the presidency. In 1900, McKinley had chosen Roosevelt as his running mate at the urging of political advisors. In 1904, it was realistic for Fairbanks not to seek the presidential nomination in the face of Roosevelt's popularity. After the 1904 convention that had nominated Fairbanks for the vice presidency, *Harper's Weekly* reported that the nomination had gone "by default to Mr. and Mrs. Fairbanks." A *Boston Post* cartoon pictured Charles Fairbanks speaking to a Republican elephant while Cornelia sat in the background presiding over a DAR meeting. The caption said, "We're just natural born Presidents in our family." An accompanying humorous poem suggested that Charles follow Cornelia's example and run for president in 1908.[45]

After his swearing-in as vice president in 1905, Fairbanks lost no time beginning his campaign for president in 1908—nor did Mrs. Fairbanks lose any time in assisting his quest for yet another office. The National Republican Editorial Association met in Washington a few days after the inaugural. Fairbanks met with them. Many of the editors were thinking favorably of a Fairbanks candidacy in 1908. President Roosevelt received the Republican editors at the White House in the afternoon. The Fairbankses entertained the editors, their wives, and daughters at a reception at their home in the evening along with a cabinet member, senators, and congressmen.[46] The *Chicago Daily Tribune* reported a year later that "persons who claim to know what is going on behind the scenes" believed that Fairbanks would very likely have a sufficient number of delegates to win at the convention. "Fairbanks is a silent, persistent, painstaking worker. He has had the presidential bee in his bonnet for many years ... many persons believe that McKinley desired to see Fairbanks succeed him in the presidential chair." In Indiana, Fairbanks's nemesis Senator Beveridge had suffered "an ignominious rout," and Fairbanks seemed certain of the support of Indiana delegates to the next Republican convention. He appeared to have the support of the Illinois delegation as well and was working in the South.[47]

Mrs. Fairbanks's earlier battles in the DAR were brought into her husband's campaign. On April 18, 1905, the *New York Times* reported that "quite unexpectedly an indirect boom for Vice President Fairbanks for the Presidency was sprung at the Congress of the Daughters of the American Revolution" at the meeting that had opened after the dedication of Continental Memorial Hall. Following a toast to outgoing President General Cornelia Fairbanks, the State Regent of Maine, Mrs. Kendall, gave a speech. Among the laudatory comments she made about Mrs. Fairbanks's work for the society, Mrs. Kendall said, "May we live to see her some time as the first lady of our land in the position she is so pre-eminently fitted to fill. But wherever her lines may fall, she will be bound to us by the tenderest ties. May she live long and prosper." Mrs. Kendall seems to have been leaving open all possibilities for the future and merely to have been wishing Mrs.

Fairbanks well. But in DAR politics as well as in the male campaigns for national office, no holds were barred. There was always plenty of opportunity for opponents to accuse Washington-based Daughters of promoting the "national" agenda for wives of national politicians. The New York City chapter's support of Mrs. Donald McLean against Midwesterner Cornelia Fairbanks in 1901 paralleled conflicts between New Yorker Roosevelt and Midwesterner Charles Warren Fairbanks.

Reporting that friends and foes alike thought the vice president to be leading the field for the 1908 Republican nomination, an opinion piece in the *New York Times* attempted to assess mixed feelings about him. In contrast to apparent iciness publicly, his personal manner made everyone feel at ease in his presence; the alleged coldness seemed "political"—he was not imaginative nor one to inspire enthusiasm about issues and policies.[48]

The *Times* pointed out that Fairbanks had not initiated legislation while in the Senate and tended to wait until debate was nearly over and then make a speech summarizing the best points that had been made by others.[49] Although not necessarily statesmanship, such an approach demonstrated classic political acumen. Fairbanks's speeches on the stump seemed better to the *Times* than his speeches in the Senate— they had more life and were more interesting (and, possibly, had more input from Nellie). In the month before the piece was published it had "become evident that he is the only candidate who has made any headway in the capture of States. Several delegations in the South and West are practically assured to him, as are at least two in New England." Describing the well-known Fairbanks hospitality, the author noted, "He and his wife dispense a delightful hospitality. There is nothing forced about it. They are natural hosts, who make their guests feel at ease from the moment the door opens." Their dinners were much more enjoyable than crowded White House receptions. Pointing out that Fairbanks had often depended on others for advancement, the article claimed that he did not keep friends for more than a few years. Since becoming a candidate, Fairbanks seemed to that particular reporter as having "improved a good deal in geniality and also in secretiveness."[50] Perhaps Charles Fairbanks did have some difficulty trusting others fully.[51] At least he seems to have played his cards close to the chest. A campaign biography noted that when talking to reporters he gave suggestions but never divulged plans; in working behind the scenes he avoided anything that could be distorted into a binding promise; and to his "corps of effective lieutenants" he "divulged just enough of his plans to put them to intelligent and earnest work."[52] Campaigning for the forthcoming presidential nomination, Fairbanks's reserved public demeanor did not serve him well in a country accustomed to the charismatic President Roosevelt and the frequent Democratic candidate and dramatic orator William Jennings Bryan. Humorists and newspaper cartoonists had a field day with the dignified Hoosier. Although some saw him as an effective public speaker, others thought the content of his talks banal. Roosevelt, himself, was not above making jokes at Fairbanks's expense. At the 1908 Republican Convention, Roosevelt, who supported Taft, seemed surprised that the candidate they would have the most trouble beating was Fairbanks. He told a delegate, "Think of it—Charley Fairbanks! ... He's got a hold in Kentucky, Indiana, and some other states that is hard to break. How and why is beyond me."[53]

When not traveling and giving speeches, Fairbanks "enjoyed his tenure as vice president. The quiescent routine of the office was made to order for him. His congenial nature made him a fair and impartial presiding officer in the Senate, and his favored financial status enabled him to meet his social obligations as Washington's official party giver. Someone suggested that he be made the country's perpetual vice president."[54]

Ohio farm boy Fairbanks was as complex as the judge's daughter he married. No one seemed to disagree that they were both skilled politicians. And everyone loved to attend social gatherings in their home. It is impossible to believe that, in Washington, D.C., they were not accomplishing many of their political goals while genuinely enjoying being delightful hosts.

Chapter Fourteen

So Many Americans Scattered Over the Earth

After leaving official Washington in March 1909, Charles and Nellie Fairbanks embarked on a world tour. The first leg of the journey was from Indianapolis to California where they and their daughter Adelaide Timmons visited their son Frederick and his family in Pasadena. The former vice president felt that he had "been tied down all my life" and welcomed "this opportunity to make a tour of the world … I do not know just where we shall go, but wherever we do, we shall take plenty of time and not follow the beaten path of travel," he predicted. They set sail from San Francisco for the Hawaiian Islands on the Japanese steamship Cheyo Maru. The Governor of the Hawaiian Territory and the Chamber of Commerce of Honolulu gave them a warm welcome.[1] Like Alaska, which they had visited earlier, these islands would not become a state for another half century. In Honolulu, Adelaide decided to return to the mainland and not to continue the trip with her parents.[2] Subsequent travels took Mr. and Mrs. Fairbanks to Japan, China, the Philippines, India, Egypt, the Holy Land, Turkey, Greece, Italy, Austria, Germany, France, and England.[3] Finally, they sailed west across the Atlantic, albeit in much better accommodations than their ancestors three centuries earlier, and landed in New York a year after their journey had begun.

The Fairbankses were traversing a world of transition where the future of the twentieth century was developing in a way that would have been unimaginable to them. President Roosevelt had won the Nobel Peace Prize for negotiating a settlement for the Russo-Japanese War that left Japan a power in the Pacific Ocean. The culmination would come a little more than three decades after the Fairbankses visited Pearl Harbor in Hawaii and Manila in the Philippines—December 7, 1941.

In Tokyo, former Vice President and Mrs. Fairbanks, presented by the American Ambassador, were received by the Emperor and Empress of Japan. The Emperor guaranteed the former vice president a warm welcome in his country and asked that he convey to Americans "an assurance of continued friendship and the ever-increasing reliance of the Japanese people upon the good will of the United States."[4]

While in Tokyo, they were guests of Japanese Prime Minister Okuma. According to custom, Mrs. Fairbanks was allowed to fish in a small stream flowing through his elaborate Japanese gardens. She caught more trout than any of the other guests. Some of the fish she caught were later prepared and served to them at dinner. In the beautiful, temple-filled, ancient capital of Kyoto, a residence owned by another wealthy Japanese gentleman was made available to the Fairbankses.[5]

The vice president attended Memorial Day Services at the American Naval Hospital in the Tokyo port of Yokohama. The weather was brilliant; Marines and sailors from the visiting American squadron formed an honor guard for the dignitaries that included Ambassador O'Brien and Admiral Harber. Numerous arrangements of flowers "filled the hospital with their fragrance."[6]

The month in Japan "was one of the most delightful of the entire twelve of their trip."[7] Japanese women likely marveled at the prerogatives of an American New Woman like Mrs. Fairbanks.

Leaving Japan, they visited Manchuria and Korea, then occupied by Japan, on the way to spend several weeks in the summer of 1909 in China. While traveling in Korea, Charles Fairbanks noted that the "political, social, and industrial" condition of Korea was improving under the Japanese protectorate. A judicial system and good schools had been established, including public medical, legal, and agricultural colleges. Foreign missionaries were working in the effort to provide colleges and universities.[8]

Almost hundred years later, in a very different century, David Halberstam wrote, "It seemed to be part of Korea's national destiny to have little say about its own future. The peacemaker in the Russo-Japanese War was not a Korean but the president of the United States, Theodore Roosevelt ... Roosevelt represented a new, ever more muscular America just beginning to manifest itself in a kind of subconscious imperialist impulse." American-educated Korean Syngman Rhee "had been chosen by some of his countrymen to visit Theodore Roosevelt in the summer of 1905 just as the president was about to negotiate the Russian-Japanese Peace Treaty. Rhee wanted Roosevelt's help in stopping Japan's colonization of his country ... even as they were talking, Secretary of State William Howard Taft was on his way to Tokyo to work out a secret treaty giving the Japanese control of Manchuria and Korea, with the Japanese in return pledging the United States a free hand in the Philippines ... Eventually, the Japanese, who renamed Korea *Chosen,* initiated a brutal colonial reign that lasted almost forty years."[9]

While spending eight weeks at Peliaho, a missionary settlement in China, the Fairbankses were able to rest and relax. They developed an "intimate knowledge of the progress of Christianity in the Orient," in which both were greatly interested. On a trip from Peking to Kaigan on a special train on the new railroad they were accompanied by a Chinese civil engineer who was a Yale graduate like two of their sons. They visited the Ming Tombs and the Great Wall where Charles obtained several bricks as souvenirs. The dignified former senator was really relaxing; he shaved off his traditional mustache and beard in China.[10] The *Christian Science Monitor* described Charles W. Fairbanks as "a magnificent missionary" who "preached the gospel of American friendship; he has kept constantly before him the possibilities for American enterprise in this great undeveloped country, and he has impressed on the Chinese the immense gains to them of cordial relations with America." To young Chinese at YMCA meetings in Shanghai, Canton, and Hong Kong, he gave inspirational speeches about "the development of character, the acquirement of western technical, commercial, and political knowledge, and an understanding of the elements of political economy, with the object of elevating the nation to the forefront of the world's powers. The young Chinese listened with rapt attention and went away with an uplift that will be incalculable future good."[11]

At the time of the Fairbanks's world tour, the trajectories of two strong trends in nineteenth-century America were crossing. One was the missionary effort, which succeeded in providing education for many in countries not then industrialized. Many of these educated elite, often imbued with respect for America's fight for independence, became fervent nationalists, putting them in conflict with another nineteenth-century American trend—a sense of Manifest Destiny and overseas intervention. China would become a world power again as it had been for centuries in the past—but not for several decades and not as an admirer of the United States.

Charles and Nellie spent the better part of October 1909 in the Philippines, a United States possession since the Spanish-American War. Because Charles had helped shape legislation in the U.S. Senate for the governance of the Philippines, he and Nellie had a special interest in observing progress there. Government vessels were placed at their disposal for cruises around the islands. Land excursions were by automobile and horse back. There were receptions in Manila and the former vice president reviewed American soldiers as well as Philippine national troops.[12] Charles Fairbanks's friend and mentor President William McKinley, as David Halberstam wrote, had had "complex and conflicting feelings about America's onrushing new role as an imperial power in the Pacific." He had been "as surprised as anyone to discover that not only was he dealing with the suppression of a Cuban insurrection but that the United States' easy success there had led to a larger and more complicated additional step in the Pacific ... the far more difficult task of imposing America's will on an indigenous uprising in Asia." Philippine nationals "wanted one thing—the Spanish imperialists gone. At first they welcomed American help, and then they found—it was part of the age—that the United States intended to do what was good for America and only then, for them as well; that is, create a new political order for them, albeit under U.S. rule and sovereignty."[13] America's first colonial experience was happy until "the brutal counterinsurgency campaign the United States fought in the Philippines heralded much of what was to happen in the coming century ... President McKinley did not particularly want the islands ... But the pressure in the United States for some form of expansion, a continuation of that nineteenth-century sense of an American Manifest Destiny and an expression of the need to display to the rest of the world America's new economic muscle, had its own momentum ... As the *Washington Post* noted, 'A new consciousness seems to have come through the Red Sea, the Gulf of Suez, and the Suez Canal to the Nile River in Egypt, which they traversed by vessel as far as the ancient city of Thebes. From Thebes they went direct to Palestine, having arranged their itinerary so as to be in Bethlehem on Christmas Eve to witness the ceremony held in the Church of the Nativity."[19] On the way to Bethlehem, they were entertained during a brief stay in Jaffa by the American agent who had been in service there thirty years earlier when Gen. and Mrs. U.S. Grant had visited. He showed Charles and Nellie the hotel register Grant had signed. They journeyed to Jerusalem by rail along with other Americans planning to attend Christmas Eve services. There, they stayed in an impressive new hotel next to the Castle of David. The castle dated to the fourteenth century but was said to contain structures built by King David himself.

Fairbanks reported, "The narrow streets, the different types of people, the camels and the donkeys, moving hither and yon with no suggestion of haste anywhere, looked like specters. As night was coming on all bore a weird aspect. We could fancy that what we looked upon was a mere repetition of scenes which had been witnessed in the same thoroughfares for countless centuries, and that in ages to come but little change would be effected in the character and customs of the people who make up the life and the masses of the Holy City."[20] It *was* a Christmas fantasy. Much would change in Jerusalem in the twentieth and early twenty-first centuries.

They drove from Jerusalem to Bethlehem to see the entry of the Latin Patriarch into the city and later returned for the midnight mass attended by people from many countries. Processions of camels seen on their way back to Jerusalem were reminders of the Christmas story. Later, driving from Jerusalem past Bethany to Jericho, the Jordan River, and the Dead Sea, they were grateful for a good road that had been built for a visit by the Emperor of Germany a few years earlier. Greek pilgrims were being baptized in the Jordan River, near where Jesus was baptized by John the Baptist. Fairbanks noted, "Upon every hand during this journey there was some object of historic association. About half way we stopped for lunch at a roadside inn kept by a jolly Greek. It is said that in this district the parable of the Good Samaritan had its origin. I asked the Greek, our host, 'Where are the thieves?' Waving his hands aloft and sweeping the horizon, he said, 'All about—all around here,' and laughed. We observed here, as elsewhere, that the natives traveling upon the road or at work in their fields usually had guns strapped upon their backs, which suggested the existence of a lawless element which time seems unable to eradicate."[21] German excavations of the narrow streets and foundations of small houses of the ancient city of Jericho were on their itinerary. Charles continued his report, "After we had visited Jerusalem and its most interesting environs, such as the Garden of Gethsemane, the Mt. of Olives and so on, we set out upon a journey by wagon northwest to Haifa, upon the Mediterranean Sea, and thence eastwardly to Nazareth, Tiberias, and the Sea of Galilee. The weather was somewhat wintry and disagreeable, yet we made the journey with comparative freedom from discomfort. [For] a part of the distance we traveled out of the beaten path, and saw the life of the natives in all its simplicity. Here and there it was apparent that the intrusion of foreigners was not greatly relished; two or three places our carriages were pelted with stones by the young hoodlum element, and at one place the officers of the law were seriously taxed to prevent embarrassing disturbance. En route we visited a number of Bedouin camps. The nomadic people who live in the tents are, of course, not very high in the scale of civilization. They and their ancestors knew nothing except this rude form of life." Later, "we met a dozen Bedouin chiefs upon their beautiful horses ... When told who we were, the leading one looked at me, smiled and said, 'America, America—much money.'"[22] Perhaps, the wealthy railroad lawyer reported this with a little irony.

When they sailed on the Sea of Galilee, a high breeze arose after dark, tossing their small boat. Reminiscent of a Biblical story of Jesus calming the same waters under similar conditions, this experience must have been a poignant moment for the Fairbankses. Fairbanks described the return journey when "we learned from the Moslems, who manned our small craft, something of the prejudice and feeling against the Jews. One of them said, with an air of pride, that he had served four months in jail for attempting to kill a Jew. The head of the crew, a big, savage-looking fellow, said, through our interpreter, that in his time he had killed four Jews and expected to kill some more. They said the Jews, owing to the feeling, did not venture out upon the streets of Tiberias after nightfall." When Fairbanks asked the interpreter if this was true, he replied, "They are a bad lot, whether they are telling the truth or not, for they either had murder upon their hands or in their hearts."[23] This, too, was an obvious portent of things to come. Almost a hundred years after the Fairbankses were there, American officials would continue to be vexed about how to deal with the region. In the twenty-first century, the concept of American Manifest Destiny was not dead, just focused elsewhere than it had been in McKinley's and Roosevelt's day.

In Damascus, "We saw some of the large mosques and the numerous bazaars which are a feature of this ancient city"; in Baalbek, they viewed "the most stupendous and interesting ruins to be found anywhere"; in Beirut, they visited the "great Syrian Protestant College supported by contributions from America [American University of Beirut]. The students of this institution were among the most active revolutionists who overthrew the old and instituted the new regime in Turkey."[24] They sailed from Beirut to Smyrna and Constantinople.

After sailing to Naples, they were met at Cassino on the way to Rome by the superintendent of the Methodist Church in Italy and the pastor of the American Methodist Church in Rome. They were to have been met at the train station in Rome by the American Ambassador, but the two parties arrived on opposite sides of the station, and embassy staff did not catch up with the vice president until they met him at the Hotel Excelsior.[25] Italian King Victor Emmanuel received Fairbanks in a private audience and expressed appreciation of American generosity after a recent earthquake in Messina.[26] In spite of this happy event in Rome, not all would be well there. Once again, as in the incident of serving cocktails to President Roosevelt in Indianapolis, Charles Fairbanks's innocent, sincere involvement with the Methodist Church would lead to trouble. Fairbanks was scheduled to have a private audience with the Pope. He had promised to give a speech to Methodist students. There had been Methodist missionaries in Rome since religious freedom had been declared in Italy in 1870. They had made converts, but their presence was not prominent until it became known that the former vice president was scheduled to speak to them.[27] Papal audience was cancelled unless Fairbanks agreed to cancel his speech to the Methodist group. He did not. The situation caused uproar among Protestants and Catholics in the United States.

The *Chicago Daily Tribune* noted that "Protestants generally warmly congratulated the former vice president, upon what they termed his dignified attitude in the matter ... The Catholics place the responsibility for the unpleasantness upon what they describe as the offensive Methodist propaganda being conducted in Rome."[28] In newspapers throughout the United States, Protestant church leaders praised Fairbanks; Catholic Bishops condemned him.

In a subsequent report, the *Tribune* presented both sides of the situation: "The Pope said [that] he regretted he had been unable to receive Mr. Fairbanks, but that he could not depart from the policy adopted, as to do so would appear to give recognition to the disloyal interference of certain Protestant denominations." Fairbanks's version: "When on Sunday I reached the American college, Mgr. Kennedy said he had been advised from the Vatican that it would be impossible for me to have a papal audience if I delivered my contemplated address at the American Methodist church. I replied that I had agreed to make an address and was obliged to keep the agreement; that I had always exercised the privilege to speak to Catholics and Protestants alike whenever they desired and whenever it was possible, and, therefore, the arrangement for the audience I regarded as ended. I spoke to the students of the American college along patriotic and moral lines, giving the Catholic Church a full share of the credit for the great work accomplished by all the Christian churches."[29] Both former Vice President Fairbanks and Pope Pius X, no strangers to politics, later issued statements that it had all been a misunderstanding by subordinates and that each of them strongly supported freedom of religious belief.[30] Fairbanks had long since put his money where his mouth was. When still in Washington, he had contributed money to the new Catholic university there.[31]

There was speculation about whether former President Roosevelt would keep a scheduled audience at the Vatican planned for his later visit to Rome. An unnamed diplomat attributed Roosevelt's failure to visit the Vatican to tactlessness and lack of diplomacy on the part of the American Ambassador to Rome.[32] In Berlin, the Fairbankses continued to be the recipients of "a constant round of hospitality. Mrs. Fairbanks says there are so many Americans scattered over the earth, and they are so hospitable, that she and her husband have hardly had time to see much of the people in the lands in which they have traveled." The American Ambassador in Berlin and his wife gave a dinner for Mr. and Mrs. Fairbanks at which many German and American dignitaries were would be lacking in loyalty toward them if he made too free use of the facts which came into his possession through the privileges extended to him."[40] Most newspaper accounts focused on Charles's visits with royalty and other heads of state. Nellie was entertained by the wives of men of high rank as well as by wives of American ambassadors. The series of articles later published in the Sunday *Indianapolis Star* along with copies of drawings, photographs, and postcards was a special endeavor. It is more than likely that Nellie contributed to this travel diary provided by her husband.

The Fairbankses were greeted by a crowd of thousands when they returned to Indianapolis, March 25, 1910. Their train was met at Union Station by Governor Marshall and other local, state, and national dignitaries; they were given a parade through downtown streets lined by cheering citizens. A women's committee received Mrs. Fairbanks. The former vice president and others gave speeches at Monument Circle in the heart of the city, and the celebration culminated in a performance at the Murat Theater at which they were guests of honor.[41]

They were home again for good after twelve years in Washington and one year abroad. Charles Warren Fairbanks had worked with both McKinley and Roosevelt in times of much more significance for the future than any of them realized. Like their fellow Americans, they were unaware of the long-term effects of the energy released as manifest destiny became imperialism. Only Charles would live to see the beginning of those effects as World War I began and the United States ultimately entered it.

With globalization in the twenty-first century, America's activities overseas have become more complex—new partners are interacting on the international scene. In 2007, while the United States was commemorating the anniversary of the Japanese attack at Pearl Harbor that resulted in America's entry into World War II, it was unobtrusively

Chapter Fifteen

Farewell Address

Mrs. Fairbanks remained active in the Daughters of the American Revolution until the end of her life. She spoke at the Twenty-first Continental Congress in April 1912, a year and a half before her death.[1]

The president general, Mrs. Matthew T. Scott, introduced her: "We have reserved the best of the feast for the last. We are happy this afternoon to have with us a former president general, during whose able administration our cornerstone was laid; when as yet our marble palace was formed only of such stuff as dreams are made of. It gives me very great pleasure to welcome and present to you Mrs. Charles Warren Fairbanks, Honorary President General." (Applause.)

Mrs. Fairbanks replied:

"It is with the utmost pleasure that I arise to greet you and to tell you how happy I am to see you, how glad I am to look into your dear, sweet eyes again, my friends. It has been a long while since I have had this pleasure and I could by no means forego it. I had been spending some weeks in the South and was coming this way to visit my daughter. I did not know that the fates had in store for me this lovely meeting, as I had for the moment forgotten that our date of meeting is in the week in which the 19th of April falls. And so when I arrived here and the people said to me, 'You are going to be at the Congress,' I was surprised that the time was near, but accepting the invitation of the President General, I have the pleasure to be with you. I have never felt so much at home with any audience as I do with this kind, the Daughters of the American Revolution and their friends. Some of you are new Daughters and new Delegates, but I see many of those I knew a few years ago and it is a joy to see you all.

"During my term of office and during the terms of office of my predecessors, the question of building a home for the Daughters of the American Revolution had been thought of. The matter of having a repository for its sacred relics had been thought of. But finally it worked around, during the term in which I stood in such close connection with you, to the determination that we should build a memorial which should not only be a home and repository, but it should be a monument to the noble men and women of the Revolution, who had hitherto lacked a monument.

"I will not say that the generals and statesmen, the Presidents, Vice-Presidents and members of the cabinet had lacked monuments, but the men of the line, the women at the spinning-wheel had never received their monument for their services rendered, without which the Revolution would have perished and the cause of freedom would have been unsupported and free government would have been still unknown.

"But the good women of the erstwhile Colonies arose in their might, and the good and true, strong men arose in their might, and now behold, in place of thirteen small Colonies, the great domain of States, the great States, the wonderful States of our Country! Some one State is now holding more people and more business, more plans and more of everything than you can imagine that men and women are interested in, than the whole thirteen Colonies were.

"Look at the great State of Illinois, the State of your President General; at the Empire State of New York, all the magnificent realm of the middle West, of these are fruit of the self-sacrifice, heroism and patriotism of the brave men and women of the Revolution.

"I am going to speak to you about the building of this Hall and all it represents. Why, this subject was my thought by day and my dream by night for a long time. I could scarcely wake up in the night but I would think about where we were going to get more money for Continental Hall. I really became quite mercenary. I remember when I was Vice-President General from the State of Indiana that I went with a lady who was then Vice-President General from the State of Michigan, Mrs. Julius C. Burrows, when appointed by the then President General, Mrs. Daniel Manning, to wait upon the Speaker of the House of Representatives to ask him for aid and encouragement in getting a site for this building. I assure you we went into it with some reluctance.

"I felt that Congress had some justification on their part in not giving this Society a site, for the other societies might say, 'You have given this to the Daughters of the American Revolution, why not give one to us?' and you know that, thanks to the patriotic feeling in our country, there are many societies something like ours, and if each should receive a place to build, bye and bye Uncle Sam would have nothing to give. I did not approve of it, but we went to see the Speaker and he did not give us any encouragement, although he was courteous and facetious and told us stories. But he made it clear to us that Congress would not give the site.

"As president general I went into the work of building Continental Hall with a great deal of pleasure. I had such magnificent women on my two Continental Hall committees. They were devoted to patriotic purposes and they came here when needed and came in the heat of summer from great distances in order to decide where we were to have our site.

"I presented to their attention—this. Some thought that building in the residence portion would be better, but you who have seen this site must wonder how anybody could have thought any other than this possible. Don't you?

"One meeting did not accomplish its purpose, and I called another meeting of the committee, and there, came to me the faithful and efficient Mrs. Crossman of New York, the brilliant and vivacious Mrs. Week of Montana, and your distinguished President General came from Illinois to help select the site for Continental Hall. I render a tribute of praise to her now for her coming and her work. And from Vermont came Mrs. Estey, earnest and devoted. Mrs. Murphy from Ohio, and Mrs. Mary S. Lockwood, prominent in every good thing done by the Daughters of the American Revolution, was indefatigable in this. It almost seems as though Continental Hall could not have been erected without the services of Mrs. William Lindsay of Kentucky, and Mrs. George M. Sternberg. It is almost invidious to mention or to single out the names of any one above the others, where all did such noble service.

"Some day I must write a story of these noble women and their work and mention the name of every one. They came to help buy the site for this Hall, and it was done. We broke the ground on the 11th of October, on the anniversary of the organizing of the Society, and then, you know, we laid the cornerstone, and then we builded the Hall, and then, it was my exquisite pleasure to stand witness and grace the occasion, and dedicate this Hall to the sacred cause of Freedom. I can have no prouder moment in all my life than that. Oh! It is such a joy to see here this splendid Hall, our memorial of patriotism, where in coming in, we are to shut out discord, envy and hatred and we are to bring in love and honor and praise.

"From this great Hall and these splendid women who come here, I expect the greatest good will come. I know it will come. I want you to work for it. There is only one thing that distresses me about it, and that is the debt of $190,000. How much is it?"

President General Scott answered, "One hundred and seventy thousand dollars. Don't speak of it."

But Mrs. Fairbanks continued, "I want to see you buckle on your armor and pay off that debt. It seems to me inharmonious to have a debt on a temple of liberty. Why, it is wrong to do it. It is not compatible with the idea of patriotism. See how your poor old mothers of the Revolution worked! Cannot you work a little bit? Do something, no matter how small, which will bring in some money to help lift the debt. I pray you to pay off your debt. You might cut off some beautiful piece of ornamentation you wear. I know with her artistic soul a 'Daughter of the American Revolution' would find it a great trial to deprive herself of a beautiful ornament, but let us do so; let us take our choicest ornaments and sell them and pay the debt on Continental Hall, if necessary.

"Although I hate this debt so badly, I am glad the Hall is finished. It is so beautiful a place that we can forgive hiring the money to pay for its completion, but it would be so much better if you would put your hands down into your purses and bring up some of your savings each year to this work. Hold up the hands of your President General and help pay for the Hall. I want you to do it, and I want to help you in the work. I am so proud of the Society and so in love with the Hall and with the great objects of the Daughters of the American Revolution that I cannot bear to see something just a little clouding it, as too much steam clouds a mirror. Don't have that debt. I beg of you on some day of this week when the President General calls on you to give, as perhaps she will call on you, to give contributions to pay this debt. I pray to you to roll up great amounts, as you did at one time when Mrs. Henry Shephard, of Chicago, Illinois, was the Chairman of the Continental Hall Committee. I remember never having had so exhilarating a day as that one on which she called for subscriptions for the Continental Hall. Why, she called for money with which to build, although they had no site, and they had no plans. They had nothing but their wishes to build this temple which we now own; and they raised money there, a great deal of it.

"Do something like that to help pay this $170,000. It is not an immense debt for 75,000 women; you can pay it. Go right at it and do it. Don't stand on the order of your doing, but proceed at once to do it. That is my counsel, and I think you can have no better counsel than that. I am exceedingly fond of seeing people earnest, energetic, enthusiastic, patriotic and devoted. All of these things are necessary in building a hall devoted to liberty. In educating the children of the foreigners who come here, you want to teach them to be worthy of the great badge of American citizenship. You want to teach your own children and your own grown-up people the reason why this Society was founded.

"Teach them to know that and teach them that wonderful and that beautiful quality of gratitude for benefits received.

"I feel as though I could talk to you all night and perhaps tire you telling you how much I think of you, and how I want you to devote yourselves to the objects of your Society. I want you not to care a single bit about offices, but pick out good women and put them in, and when you have got them in, support them and stand by them, and let your President General be a person sacred in your eyes. She is the head of the

Daughters of the American Revolution. I feel that I can say all kinds of things to you because I know you love me, and of course you could not love me if I did not love you. So you see how it is. Now I want you to have good officers and I want you to have great harmony. I want you to live such a beautiful life as a Society working for the cause of liberty, that people going by shall say, "Behold! the Daughters of the American Revolution! How beautifully they dwell in harmony!"

The following morning, in closing her report as chairman of the Continental Hall Committee, President General Scott said emphatically:

"And now, ladies, in conclusion I will say it is high time that from this platform, in the interests of this Society—for which I hold myself responsible as, for the passing hour, its supreme head—and in the interests of my successor—for whom I would fain pave a peaceful and thornless pathway—some protest of no uncertain or wavering tone should go out against the stealthy undermining of that splendid '*corp d'esprit*' [sic] which is our most powerful asset. 'A house divided against itself must fall,' and if to attain certain ends, violent means—such as have been resorted to, are to prevail—lowering to the dignity, and fatal to the prestige of our great organization—eating a canker into its very vitals—we may well exclaim, 'Ichabod, Ichabod, thy glory hath departed!'"[2]

She was quoting from the poem "Ichabod" by John Greenleaf Whittier, about betrayal, which includes the words, "Of all we loved and honored, naught save power remains."[3] Mrs. Fairbanks and Mrs. Scott had worked closely together in the past. Mrs. Scott now felt betrayed. She had been working during her presidency to pay off the debt, and it seemed to her that Mrs. Fairbanks was attacking her personally and attacking Mrs. McLean because the debt had been incurred and had not been paid. Mrs. McLean had supported Mrs. Scott's candidacy.

The *Washington Post* reported the following day, "Mrs. Scott in her report … made a vigorous reply to the attack made by Mrs. Charles Warren Fairbanks, an honorary president general, against Mrs. Donald McLean, another honorary president general, on Monday."[4] The bone of contention was Mrs. Fairbanks's "I hate this debt." President General Scott had warned, "Don't speak of it." Nellie Fairbanks spoke of it anyway. In the interim since Mrs. Fairbanks's president generalship, Mrs. McLean had been president general 1905–09 and had authorized bonds to raise the $200,000 necessary to complete Memorial Continental Hall, making it possible for the building to be nearly finished by 1909.[5] Mrs. Fairbanks would have set about fund raising to reduce the debt as she demanded of the delegates in 1912. Mrs. McLean had thought it more appropriate to issue bonds to complete the building as soon as possible. Mrs. Fairbanks did say with some grace, "Although I hate this debt so badly, I am glad the Hall is finished. It is so beautiful a place that we can forgive hiring the money to pay for its completion, but it would be so much better if you would put your hands down into your purses and bring up some of your savings each year to this work."

The somewhat rambling and repetitive comments of the formerly highly skilled public speaker occurred when former President General Fairbanks was suffering increasingly poor health. It had been twelve years since she had first been elected to the highest DAR office. She had worked tirelessly for the organization and had traveled widely. But her fiery enthusiasm for Memorial Continental Hall and fund raising for it had in no way abated. After years of opposition and criticism, as she spearheaded the building of Memorial Continental Hall, Mrs. Fairbanks seems to have come as close to publicly expressed anger as she ever did. Unfortunately, Mrs. Scott took the remarks personally and felt it imperative to defend Mrs. McLean.

Even though Mrs. Fairbanks was not the crisp, efficient presidential speaker of the past, the mention of forgetting that the DAR met in April was a bit disingenuous because the meeting dates were changed from February to April during her tenure as president general. The tone of her talk was generally gracious, but President General Scott obviously perceived mischief afoot under the surface in spite of Mrs. Fairbanks's plea to "dwell beautifully together in harmony."

Mrs. Scott's vehemence occurred in the context of an election contest similar to the earlier Fairbanks versus McLean contest. There had been the shifting alliances characteristic of all politics. Mrs. Scott had supported Mrs. Fairbanks during her presidency. Now, Mrs. Scott had run against Mrs. William Cummins Story in elections that Mrs. Scott had won with the support of Mrs. McLean.[6] Mrs. Story would succeed Mrs. Scott as Mrs. McLean had succeeded Mrs. Fairbanks. The New Women were quite able to play the political game. By now, it would be only eight years before they could vote nationally.

Whether or not Mrs. Fairbanks was aware of it, Mrs. McLean was unable to attend the Continental Congress in 1912 because of the recent death of her eldest daughter who was in her twenties. If she knew of it, Nellie Fairbanks surely joined the delegates' expression of sympathy for Mrs. McLean's grievous loss. But when it came to Memorial Continental Hall, Cornelia Cole Fairbanks minced no words. She remained "exceedingly fond of seeing people earnest, energetic, enthusiastic, patriotic and devoted." There is no better description of her own life even as she neared the end of it.

Chapter Sixteen

Final Years

The Fairbankses lived in Indianapolis after their return from the world trip in 1910. Nellie continued busily in local, state, and national DAR activities, as well as in other organizations such as the American Prison Association, an extension of her earlier work with the Indiana Board of Charities. She was able to realize her dream of building a truly magnificent home, designing and furnishing it and supervising the construction—her final building project. She would live there less than a year.

Nellie Fairbanks had always lived an extremely productive and busy existence. She managed an active social life with charm and grace and dealt with her own and her husband's hectic political activities calmly and firmly, all the while being much involved with her family. The way she lived her life seems even more remarkable because her health was at times a matter of serious concern. In view of her subsequent medical history, it is possible that illness might even have played a part in her absence from Ohio Wesleyan Female College for a couple of years as a young woman. When she was raising her young family and becoming active in Indianapolis, she privately wrote to her husband about ill health. In 1894, as her club work and Charles's political activities were becoming busier, she regretted on one occasion that her health would prevent her from traveling to New York City to be with him when he was there.[1]

She had had five children in eleven years when she was in her late twenties to late thirties. She cared for them during the many infectious illnesses of children at the time and reported her own symptoms consistent with influenza or other respiratory illnesses. In January 1898, less than a year after they had moved to Washington, Nellie's friend Dr. Mary Spink was called to Washington to evaluate her condition and reported that "quiet and careful nursing will restore Mrs. Fairbanks's health." There were "many anxious inquiries ... but only a few callers saw Mrs. Fairbanks."[2] In June 1906, Nellie was unable to join her family in Marysville to celebrate the eighty-sixth birthday of their mother because she was ill in a sanitarium in Indianapolis. She sent a congratulatory telegram, as did the vice president, who was attending commencement exercises at Ohio Wesleyan University.[3] The following March, she was "ill from the stress of Washington social life," and the vice president and his daughter, Mrs. Timmons, entertained at their Washington home. Although she had "come home from Atlantic City much benefited in health, she is still far from well and so far takes no active part in the social life of their home."[4] Atlantic City at the time was a fashionable seashore resort.

That summer, 1907, she was "living in a slumberous New England town, far from the track of travel, resting and building up her strength for the ordeal of the winter ... Last season she was compelled to fly from Washington dinners and the endless routine of the official amenities. She passed the entire season in seclusion in Atlantic City."[5] Her periods of ill health in 1906 and 1907 would have been especially difficult for both Nellie and Charles. The infamous incident when President Roosevelt was served cocktails in Indianapolis, the attacks on the vice president in muckraking magazines, and resulting negative publicity occurred during this period of time. In addition, Charles was mounting his campaign for nomination as president in 1908, and, as always, he needed Nellie's advice and support. It was no doubt difficult for her when she was not able to be at his side.

Another sorrow for Nellie during this period was the serious illness of her brother. On her way from Indianapolis to Washington, in November 1907, she stopped for a visit in Marysville. She and her sisters went to see Edward in a hospital in Columbus. Edward had liver disease as evidenced by jaundice. Treatment available at the time, including a stay at the French Lick Springs health resort in Indiana, was not sufficient to prevent his death the following February at age fifty-five.[6] In 1908, after William Howard Taft was nominated for president on the Republican ticket, Charles Fairbanks was proposed as a vice presidential candidate but "vehemently refused." The retiring vice president explained his reluctance to accept a repeat vice presidency: "I declined the honor, greatly as I esteemed it, because I wished to retire to private life, and to relieve Mrs. Fairbanks from the demands [her] place in Washington put upon her and which I feared were telling upon her health."[7] On their return from the world trip in March 1910, she appeared to be in good health. However, in December 1910, Charles was in the East, and she was visiting their son Fred and his family in Pasadena, as well as visiting a nearby hot springs health resort. Charles's frequent telegrams to her included comments like "We are happy to hear you are rested and getting on so nicely. There is much rejoicing." From the White House, "President and Mrs. Taft enquire anxiously after you." From Indianapolis, "Dick and I sent Xmas greetings to you all. Our best Xmas gift is knowledge of your splendid improvement."[8]

In 1912 and 1913, "She had not been in the best of health ... but the pressure of duties and responsibilities did not permit her the necessary opportunity for rest and recuperation."[9] Although she attended state and local meetings, she had not been able to work at DAR headquarters in the autumn of 1913—but did attend a committee meeting there.[10]

Her friend Dr. Mary Spink was among the physicians called on when Nellie was ill. Mary Spink had been employed as a nurse at the Indiana Hospital for the Insane in the 1880s and while there, completed medical training in 1887 in one of the schools that would later merge to become Indiana University School of Medicine. She subsequently served for many years on the Indiana State Board of Charities.[11] Mrs. Fairbanks had been the first woman member of that board and remained involved in related activities. Dr. Spink's mentor was Dr. William Fletcher, a reformer in the treatment of the mentally ill.[12] When Fletcher left Indiana Hospital for the Insane in 1887 and built a private sanitarium, Neuronhurst, Dr. Spink joined his staff. Fletcher died in 1907, and Dr. Spink became head of the institution.[13] A new structure for Neuronhurst was built in 1903, "a vine-covered building surrounded by flowers and shrubs" less than a mile from the center of Indianapolis. It provided care for psychiatric and neurological disorders, and if necessary, "bacteriological or microscopic laboratory tests and rigid medical attention." It was also "a haven of rest for minds and nerves and bodies that are tired from the jangling of modern civilized life." The accommodations for fifty patients included comfortable private rooms with wide verandas overlooking the grounds.[14] Before medical specialization as we know it now, Dr. Spink was both a psychiatrist and a neurologist. Her work would have included providing general medical treatment as well. Given Dr. Spink's broad medical capabilities and her friendship with Nellie Fairbanks, who would have readily turned to her, any assessment of a specific diagnosis for Nellie Fairbanks is speculative. Based on her very active life, we can assume that whatever her condition(s) was (were), illness was episodic with periods of high functioning, possibly including the years of her president generalship of the DAR. Beginning in 1906, after her term as president general had been completed, illness seems to have become more frequent. Her letters in the 1890s indicating influenza-like symptoms as well as her eventual death from pneumonia suggest a propensity to respiratory disorders, or at least exhaustion from bouts of the infectious illnesses for which there were no specific treatments then. Neuronhurst cared for bacteriological illnesses in that time before antibiotics. Her references in letters to her husband to "nervousness," her "worrisome nature," and her "habit of thinking I have a mortal illness" suggest the possibility of occasional episodes of major depression. On the other hand, Cornelia Fairbanks, who lived an incredibly busy life, might just have spent time at Neuronhurst and various health resorts because she was exhausted and "tired from the jangling of modern civilized life." Whatever the case, she certainly seems to have coped extremely well in spite of occasional ill health, and Dr. Spink's ministrations, in a time decades before modern medications, appear to have been beneficial.

Mrs. Fairbanks, characteristically, reciprocated the help given her at Neuronhurst. In July 1906, she presented a stirring address to the six young women in the graduating class of the Nurse's Training School there. She spoke enthusiastically to them about "the duties, responsibilities, and rewards of a nurse's life ... the important relation the nurse's duties bear to the physician's and [of] nurses organized during the Spanish-American War, which won them the publicly expressed approval of the War Department." She concluded, "May the best you have ever done, be the worst you will do hereafter."[15] Seven years later, after more periods of illness, Cornelia Cole Fairbanks died at her newly built mansion on October 24, 1913, after a nine-day episode of pneumonia. Dr. Spink was among three doctors in attendance. All of Nellie's children were at her bedside except Frederick, who was on his way from California to Indianapolis by train. She had five grandchildren: Warren's two daughters, Frederick's daughter and son, and Richard, Jr. Two granddaughters were named Cornelia.[16]

Hundreds came to the funeral at the Fairbankses' home and many more visited to pay last respects before the services. There were telegrams and messages from dignitaries around the country and countless elaborate arrangements of flowers.[17] Not long before funeral services were to begin, a workingman and his wife came to pay their respects. With tears in his eyes, he placed a tiny bouquet of garden flowers on the coffin. He was a gardener who had sold produce to Mrs. Fairbanks for many years.[18] In addition to state and local dignitaries of both political parties, several Methodists bishops were in attendance at the funeral, including two who had been undergraduates at Ohio Wesleyan University when Charles and Cornelia were there. One preached the sermon and another gave a prayer. Burial ceremonies at Crown Hill Cemetery in Indianapolis were private.[19] The *Indianapolis Star* published an editorial tribute remarking that "Many things good can be said about Mrs. Charles Warren Fairbanks ... but perhaps nothing is more distinctive or more descriptive of her character than the fact that she was universally liked, that in her intercourse with all classes and conditions of people she aroused friendly sentiment and personal esteem ... Social prominence, associations with the great ones of this and other nations, did not lessen but rather emphasized these characteristics. Always she remained sweet and unaffected, courteous and charming to all alike."[20] Daughters of the American Revolution felt that, more than any other, Mrs. Fairbanks had made possible the building of their magnificent new building. The flag over Memorial Continental Hall in Washington flew at half-mast.[21]

Epilogue

Nellie's magnificent mansion remains an imposing structure in Indianapolis today, housing offices of nonprofit organizations. An Indiana historical marker indicates that it was the home of Vice President Fairbanks. Just across the street is the largest children's museum in the world.[1] The Children's Museum of Indianapolis was founded by Nellie Fairbanks's friend, civic leader and DAR officer Mary Stewart Carey.[2] Two weeks before her death, Nellie Fairbanks occupied the place of honor at the Indiana State Conference of the DAR. At that meeting, Mrs. Carey made a motion, to great enthusiasm among the membership, that Mrs. Fairbanks be made a perpetual delegate to the conference.[3] Mrs. Fairbanks would be delighted that hundreds of thousands of children enjoy a museum so near her home and that the Fairbanks Foundation under the direction of her children, grandchildren, and great-grandchildren has awarded grants to the Children's Museum.

Charles Warren Fairbanks designated money in his will for a fund named for his beloved Nellie.[4] At fifty-year intervals, the accumulated interest from investment of the money would be given to a charitable cause in Indianapolis. The first distribution, over two hundred thousand dollars, was given to establish the Cornelia Cole Fairbanks Memorial Hospital, which opened its doors in May 1971. It provided new facilities for a twenty-five-year-old home for men with alcohol dependence and was, at the time, the state's only nonpublic specialized facility for the treatment and rehabilitation of patients with alcoholism. The new hospital included beds for women patients, also a first in Indiana.[5] At a subsequent location today, Fairbanks provides inpatient and outpatient services for adolescents as well as adults with substance abuse. Over the years, the not-for-profit institution has received funds from the Richard M. Fairbanks Foundation among others. In 2007, the CEO and President of Fairbanks Hospital and addiction treatment programs, Helene Cross, a woman interested in the construction of buildings for good purposes, dedicated a recovery center to Richard M. Fairbanks, III. This building includes facilities for a secondary school for adolescents recovering from alcohol and drug abuse.[6]

On June 2, 2007, the Cornelia Cole Fairbanks Chapter, National Society Daughters of the American Revolution, Indianapolis, celebrated the centennial of its founding by placing a memorial marker at the gravesite of Cornelia Cole Fairbanks in Crown Hill Cemetery, Indianapolis.[7]

Notes

Note for Quotation

Laurel Thatcher Ulrich, *Well-Behaved Women Seldom Make History* (New York: Alfred A. Knopf, 2007), 132.

Notes for Preface

1. "D.A.R. Battle Rages," *Washington Post*, April 17, 1911.

2. From 1872 to the present, about a hundred women have sought nomination as presidential candidates, fifty from the Republican or Democratic parties. Erica Falk, *Women for President: Media Bias in Eight Campaigns* (Urbana and Chicago: University of Illinois Press, 2008), 3.

3. "[A]lmost a third of voters [say] the nation isn't ready to elect a female president." "Obama Overtakes Clinton, Tied With McCain, Poll Says," Bloomberg/Los Angeles Times Poll, February 27, 2008, http://www.bloomberg.com/.

4. *2007 U.S. Congressional Directory* (Washington, D.C.: C-SPAN, 2007).

5. Charles Warren Fairbanks Will, No. 123693, March 19, 1918; Probated June 19, 1918, Indianapolis, Marion County, Indiana.

6. Anna Nicholas to Charles Warren Fairbanks, December 15, 1913, Fairbanks.mss, Manuscripts Department, The Lilly Library. Indiana University, Bloomington.

7. Mary Chomel, "Mrs. Charles Warren Fairbanks," *Madame,* October 1904, pamphlet, Indiana State Library, Indianapolis.

8. "Mrs. Fairbanks Is Dead at Home in Indianapolis," *Los Angeles Times,* October 24, 1913.

9. "Mrs. C. W. Fairbanks Dead," *Kansas City (Mo.) Star,* October 24, 1913.

10. "Mrs. C. W. Fairbanks Dies of Pneumonia," *Hartford (Conn.) Post,* October 25, 1913.

11. "Fairbanks Made the Vice Presidency an Influential Factor," *Washington Post,* March 4, 1909.

Notes for Chapter One

1. Catherine Clinton and Christine Lunardini, *The Columbia Guide to American Women in the Nineteenth Century* (New York: Columbia University Press, 2000), 22.

2. Tiffany K. Wayne, *Women's Roles in Nineteenth-Century America* (Westport, CT: Greenwood Press, 2007), 149-65.

3. Francesca Morgan, *Women and Patriotism in Jim Crow America* (Chapel Hill: University of North Carolina Press, 2005), 73.

4. Karen J. Blair, *The Clubwoman as Feminist, True Womanhood Redefined, 1868–1914,* 2nd printing (New York: Holmes & Meier Publishers, Inc., 1988).

5. Diana L. Bailey, *American Treasure: The Enduring Spirit of the DAR* (Washington, D.C.: Daughters of the American Revolution, 2007), 24.

6. Bailey, *American Treasure,* 20.

7. Bailey, *American Treasure,* 23–28.

8. Wayne, *Women's Roles,* 63–67

9. Anne Firor Scott, *Natural Allies, Women's Associations in American History* (Urbana: University of Illinois Press, 1993), 182.

10. Wayne, *Women's Roles,* 74–75.

11. Glenna Matthews, *The Rise of Public Woman, Woman's Power and Woman's Place in the United States, 1630–1970* (New York: Oxford University Press, 1992), 82.

12. Clinton and Lunardini, *Columbia Guide,* 78–79.

13. Morgan, *Women and Patriotism,* 1–17.

14. The executive committee voted to admit a black women's group from Boston organized by Josephine St. Pierre Ruffin. Scott, *Natural Allies,* 127; Massachusetts Foundation for the Humanities, http://www.mfh.org/specialprojects/shwlp/site/honorees/ruffin.html/.

15. Both Democrats and Republicans had been appealing for votes of black men in the years before the 1896 convention. In 1894–95, elections had been carried by Republicans in five former slave states—Delaware, Maryland, West Virginia, Kentucky, and Missouri. In addition, federal election laws, enacted during Reconstruction, had been repealed and the "dread of 'negro domination' in the South ended." This made it possible for the Republican convention of 1896 to be held

in a city in a former slave state, St. Louis. Charles M. Harvey, *Republican National Convention, St. Louis, June 16th. to 18th., 1896* (St. Louis, MO: I. Haas Publishing and Engraving Company, 1896), 82.

16. Wayne, *Women's Roles*, 120.

17. Morgan, *Women and Patriotism*, 90–92.

18. Mark Leibovich, "Rights vs. Rights: An Improbable Collision Course," *New York Times*, January 13, 2008.

19. Ibid.

20. Bailey, *American Treasure*, 178–79, 240–41.

21. Scott, *Natural Allies*, 111.

22. Rebecca Edwards, "Gender, Class, and the Transformation of the Electoral Campaigns in the Gilded Age," in Melanie Gustafson, Kristie Miller, and Elisabeth I. Perry, eds., *We Have Come to Stay, American Women and Political Parties, 1880-1960* (Albuquerque: University of New Mexico Press, 1999), 14.

23. Blair, *Clubwoman as Feminist*, 93–115.

24. Denise L. Baer, "Women, Women's Organizations, and Political Parties," in Susan J. Carroll, ed., *Women and American Politics* (New York: Oxford University Press, 2003), 117–19.

25. Scott, *Natural Allies*, 3.

26. Charles Warren Fairbanks Will, 123693, March 18, 1918; Probated June 19, 1918, Indianapolis, Marion County, Indiana.

27. "Mrs. Charles W. Fairbanks—'The Clubwoman of Today,'" *Cincinnati Post*, November 1, 1901.

Notes for Chapter Two

1. Biographical material about Philander B. Cole, his wife Dorothy Witter Cole, and their children in *Memorial Record of the Counties of Delaware, Union, and Morrow, Ohio* (Chicago: The Lewis Publishing Co., 1895), 377–79, and *The History of Union County, Ohio* (Chicago: W. H. Beers & Co., 1883), Facsimile Reprint (Bowie, MD: Heritage Books, Inc. in cooperation with the Union County Ohio Genealogical Society, Marysville, Ohio, 1996), Part V, 16–18, 21.

2. Catherine Clinton and Christine Lunardini, *The Columbia Guide to American Women in the Nineteenth Century* (New York: Columbia University Press, 2000), 129.

3. Tiffany K. Wayne, *Women's Roles in Nineteenth Century America* (Wesport, CT: Greenwood Press, 2007), 84.

4. Mrs. Elias J. Jacoby, *In Memory and Appreciation of Cornelia Cole Fairbanks* (Indianapolis: Caroline Scott Harrison Chapter, Daughters of the American Revolution, Nov. 13, 1913), comments about Nellie Cole's childhood and education. The Jacoby family was from Union County, Ohio, and Mrs. Jacoby's husband was later Charles Fairbanks's law partner in Indianapolis.

5. *The History of Union County*, Part V, 35.

6. *The History of Union County*, Part V, 17; P.B. Cole and underground railroad and support for Lincoln: 1958 interview with Cornelia's daughter in Herbert J. Rissler, "Charles Warren Fairbanks, Conservative Hoosier," Ph.D.

Dissertation (Indiana University: Bloomington, Indiana, 1961), 28.

7. *The History of Union County*, Part IV, 354.

8. U.S. Census, Marysville, Ohio, 1850: the Philander B. Cole family included Cornelia, age 2; U.S. Census, 1860: Cornelia, age 12; U.S. Census, 1870: Nellie, age 20. Birth dates of parents and other children were consistent in all censuses. The census taker in 1850 could not have listed Cornelia two years before she was born. That she was not just named for an older sibling who died in infancy is consistent with the 1860 Census: Cornelia, age 12. Her birth date, 1900 U.S. Census for Indianapolis, is recorded as January, 1852. Charles Fairbanks was born in May, 1852. Newspaper reference (see note 17) to her "apparent" age might just have been a nineteenth-century courteous reluctance to refer to the age of any lady; however, the reporter might have had an inkling or knowledge of her actual age.

9. She attended a female seminary in Granville, was "unsatisfied," and left after six months: *Marysville (OH) Journal Tribune,* 1969 Sesquicentennial Special Edition reprint of 1908 biographical article, Union County Historical Society, Marysville, Ohio; Alumni Records, Special Collections, Beeghly Library, Ohio Wesleyan University, Delaware, Ohio: Ohio Wesleyan Female College: 1867–68, Sophomore Class; 1868–69, housewife [presumably at home in Marysville]; Senior Class, 1871–72.

10. Jacoby, *In Memory and Appreciation.* "After graduating from the high school, she attended the Young Ladies' Seminary at Granville, Ohio for a short time, and in 1870 matriculated

at the Ohio Wesleyan Female College … Before entering college she taught in a public school for part of the term to accommodate a friend who was ill." Her teaching seems to have occurred in the year Ohio Wesleyan records list her as a "housewife" (see note 9).

11. *The History of Union County*, Part V, 18, 21.

12. Wayne, *Women's Roles*, 90: "The first woman to receive a law degree in the United States was Ada Kepley, who graduated from the Union College of Law (now Northwestern University) in Chicago in 1870."

Notes for Chapter Three

1. Mrs. Elias J. Jacoby, *In Memory and Appreciation of Cornelia Cole Fairbanks* (Indianapolis: Caroline Scott Harrison Chapter, Daughters of the American Revolution, Nov. 13, 1913). "She joined the Clionian Literary Society"; Henry Clyde Hubbart, *OHIO WESLEYAN'S First Hundred Years* (Delaware, Ohio: Ohio Wesleyan University, 1943), 51–52. The motto of the Clionian Literary Society was "Licht, Mehr Licht" ("Light, More Light," the last words of Goethe).

2. Thomas J. Brown, *DOROTHEA DIX, New England Reformer* (Cambridge: Harvard University Press, 1998), 155.

3. Caroline Field Levander, *Voices of the Nation, Women and Public Speech in Nineteenth-Century Literature and Culture* (Cambridge, UK: Cambridge University Press, 1998), 1–11, 21, 141–46.

4. Quoted in Jacoby, *In Memory and Appreciation*.

5. Quoted in *The Western Collegian,* Ohio Wesleyan University, June 12, 1872.

6. Editorial, *The Western Collegian*, October 4, 1871; comment from REP, June 12, 1872.

7. Prof. E. T. Nelson, ed., *Fifty Years of History of the Ohio Wesleyan University, Delaware, Ohio, 1844-1894* (Cleveland, OH: The Cleveland Printing and Publishing Co., 1895), 464–65.

8. *The Western Collegian,* June 12, 1872.

9. William Henry Smith, *The Life and Speeches of Hon. Charles Warren Fairbanks* (Indianapolis, IN: Wm. B. Burford, 1904), 11.

10. Ruth Neely, *Women of Ohio* (Ohio Newspaper Women's Association: S. J. Clarke Publishing Co.) 3:1051, Ohio State Library, Columbus.

11. Herbert J. Rissler, "Charles Warren Fairbanks: Conservative Hoosier," Ph.D. Dissertation (Indiana University, Bloomington, Indiana, 1961), 28.

12. Hubbart, *OHIO WESLEYAN'S First Hundred,* 55.

13. *Ohio Wesleyan Magazine*, December 1948, 58.

14. Hubbart, *OHIO WESLEYAN'S First Hundred,* 30.

15. Julius Chambers, "Obituary of Charles Warren Fairbanks," reprint from *Brooklyn Eagle* in *Ohio Wesleyan Alumni Quarterly* (July 1918): 16–17.

16. *Ohio Wesleyan Magazine,* February 1953, 57.

17. Hubbart, *OHIO WESLEYAN'S First Hundred,* 51–52.

18. Jacoby, *In Memory and Appreciation.*

19. Smith, *Life and Speeches,* 19–20.

20. Rissler, "Charles Warren Fairbanks," 28.

21. Rissler, "Charles Warren Fairbanks," 10.

22. Newspaper clipping file, Fairbanks.mss, Manuscripts Department, The Lilly Library, Indiana University, Bloomington.

23. Margaret Main Bouic, "Excerpts from the *Marysville Tribune,* 1850–1890," Union County Chapter of the Ohio Genealogical Society, 97.

Notes for Chapter Four

1. Thomas J. Schlereth, *Victorian America: Transformations in Everyday Life* (New York: Harper Collins, 1991), xi–xvi.

2. Schlereth, *Victorian America*, 304–53.

3. Mary Chomel, "Mrs. Charles Warren Fairbanks," *Madame,* October, 1904, pamphlet, Indiana State Library, Indianapolis.

4. William Henry Smith, *The Life and Speeches of Hon. Charles Warren Fairbanks* (Indianapolis, IN: Wm. G. Burford, 1904), 188–90.

5. "Mrs. C. W. Fairbanks Dead," *Boston Globe,* October 25, 1913.

6. *St. Louis Globe Democrat,* October 28, 1913.

7. Smith, *Life and Speeches*, 188.

8. Smith, *Life and Speeches*, 190.

9. Charles Warren Smith was "one of the most prominent and successful railroad officers in the United States" as general manager of the Chesapeake and Ohio. William Henry Smith

was general manager of the Western Associated Press, the "largest news organization in the world." *The History of Union County, Ohio* (Chicago: W. H. Beers & Co., 1883), Part V, 246–47.

10. Clifton J. Phillips, *Indiana in Transition: The Emergence of an Industrial Commonwealth, 1880–1920* (Indianapolis: Indiana Historical Society and Indiana Historical Bureau, 1968), 52; Leonard Schlup, "Charles Warren Fairbanks," in J. A. Garraty and M.C. Carnes, eds., *American National Biography* (New York: Oxford University Press, 1999) 7:676–77.

11. Lida B. Earhart, "Cornelia Cole Fairbanks," manuscript (Washington, D.C.: Daughters of the American Revolution, 1938), 2.

12. Chomel, "Mrs. Charles Warren Fairbanks."

13. Emma C. Piatt, *History of Piatt County,* circa 1882, second reprinting, Piatt County Historical and Genealogy Society, Monticello, IL (Evansville, IN: Whipporwill Publications, 1985), 152, 621, map of Piatt County; "How Senator Fairbanks Has Made a Great Success as a Corn Farmer," *Indianapolis News,* August 9, 1902.

14. "How Senator Fairbanks," *Indianapolis News.*

15. Cornelia Fairbanks to Charles Fairbanks, July 18, 1889, Correspondence, Fairbanks.mss, Manuscripts Department, The Lilly Library, Indiana University, Bloomington.

16. Mrs. John Lee Dinwiddie, *In Memory and Appreciation of Cornelia Cole Fairbanks* (Indianapolis, IN: Caroline Scott Harrison Chapter, Daughters of the American Revolution, Nov. 13, 1913).

17. Mrs. Chapin C. Foster, *In Memory and Appreciation*.

18. Mrs. C. E. Kregelo, *In Memory and Appreciation*.

19. Foster, *In Memory and Appreciation*.

20. "Fortnightly Literary Club 1892/1893 Program," William Henry Smith Library, Indiana Historical Society, Indianapolis.

21. "The Women Step Forward," *Indianapolis Sentinel,* May 9, 1890.

22. Front-page article by Laura A. Smith on women's clubs in Indianapolis and article, "Propylaeum," *Indianapolis Sentinel,* January 25, 1891.

23. *Indianapolis Propylaeum, Description of Building, and Account of the Dedicatory Exercises including Historical Sketch and President's Address* (Indianapolis, IN: Carlon and Hollenbeck, 1891) William Henry Smith Library, Indiana Historical Society, Indianapolis.

24. Anne Firor Scott, *Natural Allies, Women's Associations in American History* (Urbana: University of Illinois Press, 1993), 126.

25. "Fortnightly Literary Club."

26. Phillips, *Indiana in Transition,* 483–86.

27. Cornelia Fairbanks to Charles Fairbanks, April 7, 1890, Correspondence, Fairbanks.mss, Manuscripts Department, The Lilly Library, Indiana University, Bloomington.

28. Cornelia Fairbanks to Charles Fairbanks, May 19, 1890, Correspondence, Fairbanks.mss, Manuscripts Department, The Lilly Library, Indiana University, Bloomington.

29. Cornelia Fairbanks to Charles Fairbanks, November 17, 1890, Coresspondence, Fairbanks.mss, Manuscripts Department, The Lilly Library, Indiana University, Bloomington.

30. Clifton J. Phillips, *Indiana in Transition: The Emergence of an Industrial Commonwealth, 1880–1920* (Indianapolis: Indiana Historical Bureau & Indiana Historical Society, 1968), 33.

31. Phillips, *Indiana in Transition*, 37.

32. Margaret Main Bouic, *Marysville Tribune Abstracts,* February 3, 1892, Marysville Public Library, Marysville, Ohio.

33. Cornelia Fairbanks to Charles Fairbanks, December 10, 1890, Correspondence, Fairbanks.mss, Manuscripts Department, The Lilly Library, Indiana University, Bloomington,

34. Cornelia Fairbanks to Charles Fairbanks, January 11, 1894, Correspondence, Fairbanks.mss, Manuscripts Department, The Lilly Library, Indiana University, Bloomington.

35. Cornelia Fairbanks to Charles Fairbanks, January 12, 1894, Correspondence, Fairbanks.mss, Manuscripts Department, The Lilly Library, Indiana University, Bloomington.

Notes for Chapter Five

1. James H. Madison, "Charles Warren Fairbanks and Indiana Republicanism," in *Gentlemen from Indiana: National Party Candidates, 1836–1940* (Indianapolis: Indiana Historical Bureau, 1977), 176.

2. Mark O. Hatfield with the Senate Historical Office, *Vice Presidents of the United States, 1789–1993* (Washington, D.C.: U. S. Govt. Printing Office, 1977), 314.

3. Elliott Parker, "Political Power and the Press, Charles Warren Fairbanks," Association for Education in Journalism and Mass Communication, Toronto, Canada, August 2004, http://list. msu.edu/cgibin/wa?A2=ind0411c&L=aejmc&P=26977/.

4. "The First Day, without a Hitch the Great Convention Accomplishes Temporary Organization," *St. Louis Globe Democrat,* June 17, 1896.

5. Hatfield, *Vice Presidents,* 313.

6. Mrs. Elias J. Jacoby, *In Memory and Appreciation of Cornelia Cole Fairbanks* (Indianapolis, IN: Caroline Scott Harrison Chapter, Daughters of the American Revolution, Nov. 13, 1913).

7. Margaret Gibbons Wilson, *The American Woman in Transition, The Urban Influence, 1870–1920* (Westport, CT: Greenwood Press, 1979), 8.

8. "Fairbanks Made the Vice Presidency an Influential Factor," *Washington Post,* March 4, 1909.

9. Chomel, "Mrs. Charles Warren Fairbanks."

10. Herbert J. Rissler, *Charles Warren Fairbanks: Conservative Hoosier* Ph.D. Dissertation (Indiana University, Bloomington, 1961), 161–62.

11. Mark Wahlgren Summers, *Party Games: Getting, Keeping, and Using Power in Gilded Age Politics* (Chapel Hill: University of North Carolina Press, 2004), 160.

12. William Safire, "On Language: Bundling," *New York Times Magazine,* April 15, 2007.

13. Summers, *Party Games,* 161.

14. Hatfield, *Vice Presidents,* 314–15.

15. Hatfield, *Vice Presidents,* 315.

16. Rissler, "Charles Warren Fairbanks," 88–89.

17. Phillips, *Indiana in Transition,* 62–63.

18. Phillips, *Indiana in Transition,* 70–72.

19. Phillips, *Indiana in Transition,* 88–89.

20. Phillips, *Indiana in Transition,* 89.

21. Mrs. Adlai E. Stevenson, "Administration of Mrs. Charles Warren Fairbanks," *Brief History, Daughters of the American Revolution* (Washington, DC: National Society, Daughters of the American Revolution, circa 1913), 74–75.

22. Hatfield, *Vice Presidents,* 317.

23. Mary S. Lockwood and Emily Lee Sherwood, *Story of the Records, D. A. R.* (Washington: National Society of the Daughters of the American Revolution, 1906), 66–67.

24. Rissler, "Charles Warren Fairbanks," 179–80.

25. Hatfield, *Vice Presidents,* 315.

26. Rissler, "Charles Warren Fairbanks," 9–10.

27. Hatfield, *Vice Presidents,* 318.

28. "Fairbanks Made the Vice Presidency an Influential Factor," *Washington Post,* March 4, 1909.

29. Chomel, "Mrs. Charles Warren Fairbanks."

30. Ibid.

31. "Leads Among Women," *Washington Post,* July 10, 1904.

32. Chomel, "Mrs. Charles Warren Fairbanks."

33. Ibid.

34. "Ohio Wesleyan's New Head," *Washington Post,* June 23, 1905.

35. Clipping file, Fairbanks.mss, Manuscripts Department, The Lilly Library, Indiana University, Bloomington.

36. "Now Waiting Forgiveness," *Syracuse (N.Y.) Standard,* August 14, 1897.

37. "Obtains the Decree," *Fort Wayne (Ind.) Daily News,* December 9, 1902.

38. "U.S. Senator Fairbanks's Daughter to Wed an Ensign," *Newark (Ohio) Advertiser,* September 10, 1903.

39. "Senator's Daughter Married," *New York Times,* September 20, 1903.

40. John W. Timmons Scrapbook, Fairbanks Collection, William Henry Smith Library, Indiana Historical Society, Indianapolis.

Notes for Chapter Six

1. "Mrs. Fairbanks Tells of Alaska," *Marysville (Ohio) Tribune,* May 2, 1900.

2. *The History of Union County, Ohio* (Chicago: W. H. Beers & Co., 1883) Facsimile Reprint (Bowie, MD: Heritage Books, Inc. in cooperation with the Union County Ohio Genealogical Society, Marysville, Ohio, 1996), Part V, 18, footnote.

3. *Memorial Record of the Counties of Delaware, Union, and Morrow, Ohio.* (Chicago: The Lewis Publishing Co., 1895), 377.

4. *Memorial Record*, 378–79.

5. Joseph J. Ellis, *His Excellency, George Washington* (New York: Alfred A. Knopf, 2004), 3.

Notes for Chapter Seven

In the references in these notes, the organization Daughters of the American Revolution is referred to as "DAR" and is so referenced in the text. In official DAR publications, including those quoted below, "NSDAR" refers to the National Society Daughters of the American Revolution.

1. "D.A.R. Battle Rages," *Washington Post*, April 17, 1911.

2. "Two D.A.R. Caucuses," *Washington Post*, February 18, 1901.

3. "The D.A.R. Election," *New York Times*, February 20, 1901.

4. Minutes of the Tenth Annual Continental Congress, NSDAR, *American Monthly Magazine*, XVIII (1901): 642.

5. Lida B. Earhart, "Cornelia Cole Fairbanks," manuscript (Washington, D.C.: NSDAR, 1938).

6. Francesca Morgan, *Women and Patriotism in Jim Crow America* (Chapel Hill: The University of North Carolina Press, 2005), 63.

7. "Women Meet in Congress," *New York Times*, February 22, 1898.

8. "Daniel Manning Marries," *New York Times*, November 20, 1884.

9. Minutes of the Tenth Annual Continental Congress, NSDAR, *American Monthly Magazine*, XVIII (1901): 633–35, 638–39. 690, 694–98.

10. D.A.R. Scrapbooks, December 1900–May 1901, Fairbanks. mss, The Lilly Library, Indiana University, Bloomington.

11. Mary Chomel, "Mrs. Charles Warren Fairbanks," *Madame,* October 1904, pamphlet, Indiana State Library, 3.

Notes for Chapter Eight

1. Minutes of the Eleventh Continental Congress, NSDAR *American Monthly Magazine,* XX (1902): 714–17, 725.

2. Minutes of the Eleventh Continental Congress, 728.

3. Lida B. Earhart, *Cornelia Cole Fairbanks* (Washington, DC: NSDAR, 1938), 13.

4. Minutes of the Eleventh Continental Congress, NSDAR *American Monthly Magazine,* XX, (1902): 746–48.

5. Rhea, "Daughters in Session," *New Haven (Conn.) Evening Leader,* February 20, 1902.

6. Mary Chomel, "Mrs. Charles Warren Fairbanks."

7. Cornelia Cole Fairbanks to Charles Warren Fairbanks, May 9, 1890; January 11, 1894, Correspondence, Fairbanks.mss, Lilly Library, Indiana University, Bloomington.

8. Mary S. Lockwood and Emily Lee Sherwood, *Story of the Records D.A.R.* (Washington, DC: NSDAR, 1906), 102–3.

9. Lockwood and Sherwood, *Story of the Records,* 104.

10. Earhart, *Cornelia Cole Fairbanks,* 4,11. Ibid.

11. Mrs. Adlai E. Stevenson, "Administration of Mrs. Charles Warren Fairbanks," *Brief History, Daughters of the American Revolution* (Washington, DC: NSDAR, circa 1913), 80.

12. "Daughters Take Action in Philadelphia Row," *New York Times,* April 23, 1904.

13. Minutes of the Eleventh Continental Congress, NSDAR *American Monthly Magazine,* XX (1902): 648–57.

14. Minutes of the Eleventh Continental Congress, NSDAR *American Monthly Magazine,* XX (1902): 777.

15. Minutes of the Eleventh Continental Congress, NSDAR *American Monthly Magazine,* XX (1902): 774.

16. Minutes of the Eleventh Continental Congress, NSDAR *American Monthly Magazine,* XX (1902): 880.

17. Minutes of the Eleventh Continental Congress, NSDAR *American Monthly Magazine,* XX (1902): 915–7.

18. Minutes of the Eleventh Continental Congress, NSDAR *American Monthly Magazine,* XX (1902): 1479.

19. "Money Flows into Treasury of D.A.R.," *Washington Times,* February 22, 1902.

20. Minutes of the Eleventh Continental Congress, NSDAR *American Monthly Magazine,* XX (1902): 1132–33.

21. Minutes of the Twelfth Continental Congress, NSDAR *American Monthly Magazine,* XXII (1903): 728.

Notes for Chapter Nine

1. DAR Scrapbook, Charles Warren Fairbanks collection, William Henry Smith Library, Indiana Historical Society, Indianapolis.

2. "D. A. R. at Buffalo," *Syracuse (N.Y.) Standard,* May 31, 1901.

3. "Triumph for Mrs. M'Lean," *New York Press,* July 9, 1901.

4. "Mrs. Fairbanks Decries Anarchy," *Chicago Inter Ocean,* October 27, 1901.

5. "Daughters of the American Revolution of Georgia in Session," *Augusta Chronicle,* November 22, 1901.

6. Robert Fairbanks diaries, Fairbanks.mss, Manuscripts Department, The Lilly Library, Indiana University, Bloomington.

7. NSDAR *American Monthly Magazine,* XXII (1903): 726.

8. NSDAR *American Monthly Magazine,* XX (1902): 573–78.

9. NSDAR *American Monthly Magazine,* XXVI (1905): 102–5.

10. "In Memory of Lafayette," *Rockville (CT) Journal,* June 13, 1902.

11. "Honor to the Heroes of 1776," *Syracuse (NY) Evening Herald,* June 17, 1902.

12. Barbara J. Howe, "Women in the Nineteenth-Century Preservation Movement," in Gail Lee Dubrow and Jennifer B. Goodman, eds., *Restoring Women's History Through Historic Preservation* (Baltimore, MD: The Johns Hopkins University Press, 2003), 28, 31.

13. Lida B. Earhart, "Cornelia Cole Fairbanks," manuscript (Washington, D.C.: National Society Daughters of the American Revolution, 1938), 6–7.

14. Earhart, "Cornelia Cole Fairbanks," 5–6.

15. "On Continental Hall," *Washington Post,* April 7, 1905.

16. "Ranks Rent by a Revolt," *New York Morning Telegraph,* January 13, 1901.

17. H. Gilson Gardner, "Washington Gossip," *Chicago Journal,* February 25, 1902.

18. "Hair Pulling in Earnest," *Fort Wayne (Ind.) News,* April 19, 1905.

19. "Women's Work for Patriotic Ideals," *Philadelphia Press,* June 29, 1902.

20. "Annapolis Junior Republic," *Washington Times,* October 12, 1924.

21. William R. George and Lyman Beecher Stowe, *Citizens Made and Remade, An Interpretation of the Significance and Influence of George Junior Republics* (Boston, MA: Houghton Mifflin Company, 1912), 30.

22. George and Stowe, *Citizens Made and Remade*, 2.

23. Courtlandt Churchill Van Vechten, Jr., "A Study of the Success and Failure of One Thousand Delinquents Committed to a Boy's Republic," Ph.D. Dissertation, (Chicago: University of Chicago, 1939). He followed up 1,000 boys in a Michigan boys' republic from one to seven years. Based on parole officers' records, about 40 percent were not classified as either success or failure. Not quite half of those who could be classified were classified as successes.

24. "Annapolis Junior Republic," *Washington Times,* October 12, 1924.

Notes for Chapter Ten

1. Tiffany K. Wayne, *Women's Roles in Nineteenth-Century America* (Westport, CT: Greenwood Press, 2007), 124.

2. Louisiana Purchase Exposition Scrapbook, Louisiana Purchase Exposition collection, 197, Missouri Historical Society, St. Louis.

3. Katherine T. Corbett, *In Her Place, A Guide to St. Louis Women's History* (St. Louis: Missouri Historical Society Press, 1999), 176–78.

4. Ibid.

5. *World's Fair Bulletin* (November 1903): 20, Missouri Historical Society Library, St. Louis.

6. "D.A.R.'s to Celebrate Day," *St. Louis Post-Dispatch,* June 12, 1904.

7. "Fairbanks Likely to Win against President's Wish," *St. Louis Post-Dispatch,* June 19, 1904.

8. "Congratulations for Senator Fairbanks," *The Chicago Inter Ocean,* June 24, 1904.

9. "Indiana Nominee Has a Busy Day," *Indianapolis News,* June 24, 1904.

10. "Fairbanks Shuns the Convention," *Chicago Daily Tribune,* June 24, 1904.

11. "Men and Women of National Fame Whose Faces Are Growing Familiar in Chicago," *The Chicago Inter Ocean,* June 22, 1904.

12. "Going Home in Triumph," *Chicago Daily Tribune,* June 25, 1904.

13. "Ovation Is Given at Home of Fairbanks," *Indianapolis Star,* June 16, 1904.

14. "D.A.R. to Meet on Anniversary of the Society's Organization," *St. Louis Republic,* October 11, 1904.

15. "No Factions in D.A.R. Sessions," *St. Louis Globe-Democrat,* October 12, 1904.

16. "Mrs. Fairbanks Stops D.A.R. Row," *St. Louis Post-Dispatch,* October 10, 1904.

17. Rose Marion, "Wife of Roosevelt's Running Mate Thinks Politics 'Good Fun,'" *St. Louis Post-Dispatch,* October 11, 1904.

18. Ibid.

19. Ibid.

20. "No Factions in D.A.R. Sessions," *St. Louis Globe-Democrat,* October 12, 1904.

Notes for Chapter Eleven

1. Mary S. Lockwood and Emily Lee Sherwood, *Story of the Records D. A. R.* (Washington, D.C.: National Society Daughters of the American Revolution, 1906), 103.

2. Mrs. Adlai E. Stevenson, *Brief History Daughters of the American Revolution* (Washington, D.C.: NSDAR, circa 1913), 74.

3. Minutes of the Eleventh Continental Congress NSDAR *American Monthly Magazine,* XX (1902): 1294–95.

4. Lockwood and Sherwood, *Story of the Records,* 103.

5. Stevenson, *Brief History,* 75.

6. Lida B. Earhart, *Cornelia Cole Fairbanks* (Washington, DC: NSDAR, 1938), 9.

7. Myrtle Barker, "My Window," *Indianapolis News,* June 27, 1966.

8. "No Other Candidate," *Washington Post,* February 26, 1903.

9. NSDAR *American Monthly Magazine,* XXI (1902): 354–55.

10. NSDAR *American Monthly Magazine,* XXI (1902): 355.

11. Earhart, *Cornelia Cole Fairbanks,* 10.

12. Stevenson, *Brief History,* 76–77.

13. "No Other Candidate," *Washington Post,* February 26, 1903.

14. Ibid.

15. Ibid.

16. Ibid.

17. Earhart, *Cornelia Cole Fairbanks,* 11.

18. Stevenson, *Brief History,* 77.

19. "Our Presidents General in Miniature," D. A. R. *National Historical Magazine,* 74 (October 1940): 33.

20. Earhart, *Cornelia Cole Fairbanks,* 11.

21. Diana L. Bailey, *American Treasure: The Enduring Spirit of the DAR* (Virginia Beach, VA: The Donning Company Publishers, 2007), 35.

22. "Memorial Continental Hall," NSDAR *American Monthly Magazine,* 25 (July-December 1904): 343–46.

23. Ibid.

24. Mollie Somerville, *Washington Landmark, A View of the DAR, The Headquarters, History, and Activities, 1890–1976* (Washington, D.C.: NSDAR, 1976), 13.

Notes for Chapter Twelve

1. Lida B. Earhart, *Cornelia Cole Fairbanks* (Washington, D.C.: NSDAR, 1938), 12. The quotation is from a well-known poet of the day, Henry Van Dyke, "Inscriptions for a Friend's House" http://www.poemhunter.com/poem/inscriptions-for-a-friend-s-house/.

2. Mary S. Lockwood and Emily Lee Sherwood, *Story of the Records D. A. R.* (Washington, D.C.: NSDAR, 1906), 86–87.

3. Thomas J. Schlereth, *Victorian America: Transformations in Everyday Life, 1876–1915*, The Everyday Life in America Series (New York: Harper Perennial, 1992), 11.

4. Schlereth, *Victorian America*, 248–49.

5. William Henry Smith, *The Life and Speeches of Hon. Charles Warren Fairbanks* (Indianapolis, IN: Wm. B. Burford, 1904), 110–14.

6. "DAR Memorial Continental Hall," *Washington Post*, April 18, 1905.

7. Stevenson, *Brief History*, 80–81.

Notes for Chapter Thirteen

1. "Fairbanks Part in Day," *Chicago Daily Tribune*, March 5, 1905.

2. Herbert J. Rissler, "Charles Warren Fairbanks: Conservative Hoosier," Ph.D. dissertation (Indiana University, 1961), 4–5.

3. "In Senate Chamber," *Washington Post*, March 5, 1905.

4. Mark O. Hatfield with the Senate Historical Office, *Vice Presidents of the United States, 1789–1993* (Washington: U. S. Govt. Printing Office, 1977), 316.

5. *Illustrated Inaugural History*, Printed Political Material III, Box 74, Fairbanks.mss, Manuscripts Department, The Lilly Library, Indiana University, Bloomington,15.

6. Rissler, "Charles Warren Fairbanks," 161–62.

7. "Handsome Gowns Worn at the Ball," *Chicago Daily Tribune,* March 5, 1905.

8. "At Vice President's Home," *Washington Post,* March 7, 1905.

9. "Fairbanks Addresses the Railway Congress," *New York Times,* May 5, 1905.

10. "Fairbanks on Caste," *New York Times,* October 6, 1906.

11. "Defines His View, Fairbanks Tells Position on Labor," *Los Angeles Times,* February 4, 1907.

12. "Degree for Mr. Fairbanks," *Washington Post,* June 15, 1905.

13. "Fairbanks 'Dr.'; Harris 'Prexy,'" *Chicago Daily Tribune,* June 21, 1907.

14. Hatfield, *Vice Presidents,* 316.

15. "Roosevelt and Fairbanks, From Leslie's Weekly," *Washington Post,* June 25, 1905.

16. Ibid.

17. Hatfield, *Vice Presidents,* 316–18.

18. Kevin Phillips, *William McKinley,* Times Books American Presidents Series (New York: Henry Holt and Company, 2003), 31.

19. "Makes for Peace," *Boston Daily Globe,* March 19, 1905.

20. "Fairbanks Praises Peace," *New York Times,* July 5, 1905.

21. "Commerce of Nation," *Washington Post,* August 4, 1905.

22. Louis Auchincloss, *Theodore Roosevelt,* Times Books American Presidents Series (New York: Henry Holt and Company, 2001), 55–60.

23. "Irrigation Congress Opens at Boise City," *Los Angeles Times,* September 4, 1906.

24. "Hoosierdom Does Honor to Fairbanks," *Louisville Times,* March 31, 1918.

25. "Frederick C. Fairbanks, News President, Dies in California after a Lingering Illness," *Indianapolis News,* May 24, 1940.

26. "Cupid Outwits Fairbanks," *Chicago Daily Tribune,* October 12, 1906.

27. "Amused at Son's Marriage," *New York Times*, October 13, 1906.

28. "Fairbanks Left Springfield When He Heard of Indictment," *Newark (Ohio) Daily Advocate,* January 17, 1907.

29. Personal Scrapbook, September 6 to December 31, 1908, Charles Warren Fairbanks Collection, William Henry Smith Library, Indiana Historical Society, Indianapolis.

30. "Great Gathering Here of Leading Churchmen," *New York Times,* September 9, 1905.

31. Rissler, "Charles Warren Fairbanks," 10.

32. Ray Boomhower, "The Fatal Cocktail," *TRACES of Indiana and Midwestern History* 7 (Winter 1995):12–19.

33. Ibid.

34. Rissler, "Charles Warren Fairbanks," 191–92.

35. "Women Beat Fairbanks," *New York Times,* September 29, 1907.

36. "Cocktail Mystery Solved," *New York Times,* October 11, 1907.

37. Boomhower, "Fatal Cocktail," 19.

38. Boomhower, "Fatal Cocktail," 17.

39. Rissler, "Charles Warren Fairbanks," 33.

40. Rissler, "Charles Warren Fairbanks," 60.

41. Elliott Parker, "Political Power and the Press," *Association for Education in Journalism and Mass Communication,* Toronto, Canada, August 2004, http://list.msu.edu/cgi- bin/wa?A2=in d0411c&L=aejmc&P=26977/.
Articles referenced: David Graham Phillips, "Treason of the Senate," *Cosmopolitan,* 42 (November 1906):77–84; Gilson Gardner, "The Real Mr. Fairbanks," *Collier's Weekly* 39 (June 1, 1907):13–16; (July 13, 1907): 14–15, 26.

42. Rissler, "Charles Warren Fairbanks," 200.

43. Rissler, "Charles Warren Fairbanks," 193–94.

44. "Fairbanks Talks in South," *New York Times,* March 23, 1905.

45. Rissler, "Charles Warren Fairbanks," 161–62.

46. "Press for Fairbanks," *Washington Post,* March 9, 1905.

47. "Fairbanks Boom Looms Up Well," *Chicago Daily Tribune,* February 5, 1906.

48. "Vice-President Fairbanks Leads in the Campaign to Succeed Roosevelt," *New York Times,* February 17, 1907.

49. Ibid.

50. Ibid.

51. "Fairbanks never accepted the prevailing theories of imperialism supported by many within his own party … but his opposition stemmed more from his distrust of foreign peoples." Rissler, Charles Warren Fairbanks, 98. "He was always cautious to avoid any commitment in the fear that this would only lose him the support of those who disagreed." Rissler, "Charles Warren Fairbanks," 179.

52. William Henry Smith, *The Life and Speeches of Hon. Charles Warren Fairbanks,* (Indianapolis, IN: Wm. G. Burford, 1904), 28–29.

53. Hatfield, *Vice Presidents,* 319–20.

54. Rissler, "Charles Warren Fairbanks," 214.

Notes for Chapter Fourteen

1. "Fairbanks to Cross Pacific," *Los Angeles Times,* April 7, 1901.

2. "Mrs. Timmons Faces Fine," *Washington Post,* May 27, 1909.

3. "Around the World with Mr. and Mrs. Fairbanks," *Indianapolis Star Sunday Magazine Section,* June 19–July 24, 1910.

4. "Royal Honors for Fairbanks," *Los Angeles Times,* June 1, 1909.

5. "Around the World," *Indianapolis Star,* June 19, 1910.

6. "Royal Honors for Fairbanks," *Los Angeles Times,* June 1, 1909.

7. "Around the World," *Indianapolis Star,* June 19, 1910.

8. "Need Honesty and Learning," *Los Angeles Times,* June 27, 1909.

9. David Halberstam, *The Coldest Winter, America and the Korean War* (New York: Hyperion, 2007), 64–66.

10. "Around the World," *Indianapolis Star,* June 26, 1910.

11. "Ex-Vice-President Fairbanks Booms America in China," *Christian Science Monitor,* December 13, 1909.

12. "Around the World," *Indianapolis Star,* July 3, 1910.

13. Halberstam, *Coldest Winter,* 109.

14. Ibid.

15. "Fairbanks Declines to Act as Critic," *New York Times,* February 27, 1910.

16. "Around the World," *Indianapolis Star,* July 10, 1910.

17. Ibid.

18. Mrs. C. E. Kregelo in *In Memory and Appreciation of Cornelia Cole Fairbanks* (Indianapolis, Ind.: Caroline Scott Harrison Chapter, Daughters of the American Revolution, Nov. 13, 1913).

19. "Around the World," *Indianapolis Star,* July 17, 1910.

20. Ibid.

21. Ibid.

22. Ibid.

23. Ibid.

24. Ibid.

25. "King Receives Fairbanks," *Washington Post,* February 6, 1910.

26. Ibid.

27. "The Methodists in Rome and Their Leader," *New York Times,* April 10, 1910.

28. "Laud Action of Fairbanks," *Chicago Daily Tribune,* February 8, 1910.

29. "Pope on Fairbanks Affair," *Chicago Daily Tribune,* February 10, 1910.

30. "Fairbanks Now Sustains Pope," *Los Angeles Times,* February 11, 1910.

31. "Gibbons Fund Contributors," *New York Times,* June 17, 1905.

32. "Diplomat's View of the Roman Situation," *New York Times,* April 10, 1910.

33. "Many Affairs for Fairbanks," *Washington Post,* February 20, 1910.

34. "Fairbanks to See Kaiser," *New York Times,* February 22, 1910; February 23, 1910.

35. "Fairbankses Due in France Today," *Christian Science Monitor,* February 21, 1910.

36. "Paris Smiles over Fairbanks Photos," *New York American,* April 10, 1910.

37. "The King, the Peers, and Commons," *New York Post,* April 2, 1910.

38. "Received with Warmth by King of England," *Atlanta Georgian,* March 10, 1910.

39. "Fairbanks Declines to Act as Critic," *New York Times,* February 27, 1910.

40. Ibid.

41. "Thousands Attend 'Welcome' Parade," *Indianapolis Star,* March 25, 1910.

42. *BBC World News,* radio broadcast, December 6, 2007.

Notes for Chapter Fifteen

1. Minutes of the Twenty-first Continental Congress, NSDAR, *Proceedings of the National Society* (1912), 22.

2. Minutes of the Twenty-first Continental Congress, NSDAR, 33.

3. http://www.poemhunter.com/poem/ichabod/.

4. "Renews D.A.R. Row," *Washington Post,* April 17, 1912.

5. Mrs. James Andrew Williams, *The Wide Blue Ribbon* (Washington, D.C.: Daughters of the American Revolution, 1983), 22.

6. "Fight to Head D.A.R.," *Washington Post,* November 30, 1909.

Notes for Chapter Sixteen

1. Cornelia Fairbanks to Charles Fairbanks, January 11, 1894, Correspondence, Fairbanks.mss, Manuscript Department, The Lilly Library, Indiana University, Bloomington.

2. "Mrs. Fairbanks Better," *Fort Wayne (Ind.) Journal,* January 27, 1898.

3. Untitled, *Marysville (Ohio) Tribune,* June 13, 1906.

4. "Mrs. Fairbanks Ill from Stress of Washington Social Life," *Newark (Ohio) Daily Advocate,* March 7, 1907.

5. "Mrs. Charles W. Fairbanks, Wife of the Vice President Is a Representative American Woman in the Broadest Sense of the Term," *Washington Post,* August 4, 1907.

6. "Mrs. Fairbanks Visited Relatives in Marysville on Her Way to the National Capital," *Marysville Evening Tribune,* November 19, 1907.

7. Herbert J. Rissler, "Charles Warren Fairbanks: Conservative Hoosier," Ph.D. dissertation (Indiana University, 1961), 213–14.

8. Night Letters, December 9, 1910; December 10, 1910; December 24, 1910, mementoes from California, BV1162, Charles Warren Fairbanks Collection, William Henry Smith Library, Indiana Historical Society, Indianapolis.

9. "The Death of Mrs. C. W. Fairbanks," *Western Christian Advocate, Cincinnati, Ohio,* October 29, 1913.

10. "President-General of D.A.R. Lauds Life and Work of Mrs. Fairbanks," *Indianapolis Star,* October 27, 1913.

11. "Dr. Mary Angela Spink, 75, Dies; President of Fletcher Sanitarium," *Indianapolis Star,* September 7, 1939.

12. Lucy Jane King, *From Under the Cloud at Seven Steeples: The Peculiarly Saddened Life of Anna Agnew at the Indiana Hospital for the Insane, 1878–1883* (Zionsville, IN: Guild Press/Emmis Publishing, 2002), 95–97.

13. "Dr. Mary Angela Spink, Dies," *Indianapolis Star,* September 7, 1939.

14. "Neuronhurst Is Well Known Sanitarium," *Indianapolis News,* September 18, 1926.

15. "Address for Nurses," *Indianapolis Star,* July 8, 1906.

16. "Mrs. C. W. Fairbanks Is Dead of Pneumonia," *Indianapolis News,* October 24, 1913.

17. "Pay Last Tribute to Mrs. Fairbanks," *Indianapolis News,* October 27, 1913.

18. Ibid.

19. "Funeral Services for Mrs. C. W. Fairbanks," *Indianapolis News,* October 25, 1913.

20. Editorial, *Indianapolis Star,* October 25, 1913.

21. "Mourn Death of Mrs. Fairbanks," *Washington Times,* October 25, 1913.

Notes for Epilogue

1. http://www.childrensmuseum.org/.

2. Michelle D. Hale, "Mary Stewart Carey," in David J. Bodenhamer and Robert G. Barrows, eds., *The Encyclopedia of Indianapolis* (Bloomington: Indiana University Press, 1994), 385.

3. Mrs. Samuel Elliott Perkins in *In Memory and Appreciation of Cornelia Cole Fairbanks* (Indianapolis, IN: Caroline Scott Harrison Chapter, Daughters of the American Revolution, Nov. 13, 1913).

4. Charles Warren Fairbanks Will, No.123693, March 19, 1918; Probated June 19, 1918, Indianapolis, Marion County, Indiana.

5. "Alcoholics Hospital to Get $200,000 Fairbanks Grant," *Indianapolis Star,* December 13, 1971.

6. *Dedication Ceremony,* Recovery Center, Fairbanks, Indianapolis, Indiana, September 21, 2007.

7. *Centennial Celebration,* 4-017-IN, National Society Daughters of the American Revolution, Indianapolis, Indiana, 1901–2007, June 2, 2007.

Selected Bibliography

The following resources made important contributions to my understanding of the life and times of Cornelia Cole Fairbanks and Charles Warren Fairbanks.

Baer, Denise L. "Women, Women's Organizations, and Political Parties." In Susan J. Carroll, ed. *Women and American Politics.* New York: Oxford University Press, 2003.

Bailey, Diana L. *American Treasure: The Enduring Spirit of the DAR.* Washington, D.C.: Daughters of the American Revolution, 2007.

Blair, Karen J. *The Clubwoman as Feminist, True Womanhood Redefined, 1868–1914.* 2nd printing. New York: Holmes & Meier Publishers, Inc., 1988.

Boomhower, Ray. "The Fatal Cocktail." *TRACES of Indiana and Midwestern History* 7 (Winter 1995):12–19.

Bouic, Margaret Main. *Genealogical and Historical Records of Delaware and Union Counties.* Vol. CLE-CON. Marysville Public Library, Marysville, Ohio.

Chomel, Mary. "Mrs. Charles Warren Fairbanks." *Madame.* October 1904. Pamphlet, Indiana State Library, Indianapolis.

Clinton, Catherine and Christine Lunardini. *The Columbia Guide to American*

Women in the Nineteenth Century. New York: Columbia University Press, 2000.

Earhart, Lida B. "Cornelia Cole Fairbanks." Manuscript. Washington, D.C.: Daughters of the American Revolution, 1938.

Edwards, Rebecca. "Gender, Class, and the Transformation of the Electoral Campaigns in the Gilded Age." In Melanie Gustafson, Kristie Miller, and Elisabeth I. Perry, eds. *We Have Come to Stay, American Women and Political Parties, 1880–1960.* Albuquerque: University of New Mexico Press, 1999.

George, William R. and Lyman Beecher Stowe. *Citizens Made and Remade, An Interpretation of the Significance and Influence of George Junior Republics.* Boston, MA: Houghton Mifflin Company, 1912.

Hatfield, Mark O., with the Senate Historical Office. *Vice Presidents of the United States, 1789-1993.* Washington: U.S. Govt. Printing Office, 1977.

History of Union County, Ohio. Chicago: W. H. Beers & Co., 1883. Facsimile reprint. Bowie, MD: Heritage Books, Inc., in cooperation with the Union County Ohio Genealogical Society, Marysville, Ohio, 1996. Part V.

Howe, Barbara J. "Women in the Nineteenth-Century Preservation Movement." In Gail Lee Dubrow and Jennifer B. Goodman, eds. *Restoring Women's History through Historic Preservation.* Baltimore, MD: The Johns Hopkins University Press, 2003.

Hubbart, Henry Clyde. *OHIO WESLEYAN'S First Hundred Years.* Delaware, OH: Ohio Wesleyan University, 1943.

In Memory and Appreciation of Cornelia Cole Fairbanks. Indianapolis, IN: Caroline Scott Harrison Chapter, Daughters of the American Revolution, Nov. 13, 1913.

Levander, Caroline Field. *Voices of the Nation, Women and Public Speech in Nineteenth-Century Literature and Culture.* Cambridge, UK: Cambridge University Press, 1998.

Lockwood, Mary S. and Emily Lee Sherwood. *Story of the Records, D. A. R.* Washington: National Society of the Daughters of the American Revolution, 1906.

Madison, James H. "Charles Warren Fairbanks and Indiana Republicanism." In *Gentlemen from Indiana: National Party Candidates, 1836–1940.* Indianapolis: Indiana Historical Bureau, 1977.

Matthews, Glenna. *The Rise of Public Woman, Woman's Power and Woman's Place in the United States, 1630–1970.* New York: Oxford University Press, 1992.

Memorial Record of the Counties of Delaware, Union, and Morrow, Ohio. Chicago: The Lewis Publishing Co., 1895.

Morgan, Francesca. *Women and Patriotism in Jim Crow America.* Chapel Hill: University of North Carolina Press, 2005.

Nelson, Prof. E. T., ed. *Fifty Years of History of the Ohio Wesleyan University, Delaware, Ohio, 1844–1894.* Cleveland, OH: The Cleveland Printing and Publishing Co., 1895.

Parker, Elliott. "Political Power and the Press, Charles Warren Fairbanks." Association for Education in Journalism and Mass Communication. Toronto, Canada. August 2004. http://list.msu.edu/cgibin/wa?A2=ind0411c&L=aejmc&P=26977/.

Phillips, Clifton J. *Indiana in Transition: The Emergence of an Industrial Commonwealth, 1880–1920.* Indianapolis: Indiana Historical Society and Indiana Historical Bureau, 1968.

Phillips, Kevin. *William McKinley.* Times Books American Presidents Series. New York: Henry Holt and Company, 2003.

Rissler, Herbert J. "Charles Warren Fairbanks: Conservative Hoosier," Ph.D. dissertation. Indiana University, Bloomington, Indiana, 1961.

Schlereth, Thomas J. *Victorian America: Transformations in Everyday Life.* New York: Harper Collins, 1991.

Scott, Anne Firor. *Natural Allies, Women's Associations in American History.* Urbana: University of Illinois Press, 1993.

Smith, William Henry. *The Life and Speeches of Hon. Charles Warren Fairbanks.* Indianapolis, IN: Wm. B. Burford, 1904.

Stevenson, Mrs. Adlai E. "Administration of Mrs. Charles Warren Fairbanks." In *Brief History, Daughters of the American Revolution.* Washington, DC: National Society, Daughters of the American Revolution, circa 1913. Chapter X.

Summers, Mark Wahlgren. *Party Games: Getting, Keeping, and Using Power in Gilded Age Politics.* Chapel Hill: University of North Carolina Press, 2004.

Wayne, Tiffany K. *Women's Roles in Nineteenth Century America.* Westport, CT: Greenwood Press, 2007.

Wilson, Margaret Gibbons, *The American Woman in Transition, The Urban Influence, 1870–1920.* Westport, CT: Greenwood Press, 1979.

List of Illustrations

1. West Union School where Nellie Cole completed her education at public school. Her father was on the first school board of Union County, Ohio. Union County Ohio Historical Society.

2. Judge Philander B. Cole, Marysville, Union County, Ohio 1815–1892, father and mentor of Cornelia Cole Fairbanks. Union County Ohio Historical Society.

3. Yearbook picture, Cornelia Cole, Ohio Wesleyan Female Seminary, 1872. Ohio Wesleyan University Historical Collection.

4. Monnett Hall, Ohio Wesleyan Female College: Cornelia Cole graduated from college here in 1872. The female college became part of its brother institution, Ohio Wesleyan University, five years later. Ohio Wesleyan University Historical Collection.

5. Union County Courthouse, Marysville, Ohio. Judge Cole practiced here in his later years. David Ficko photo.

6. Union Block, Marysville, Ohio. Judge Cole's last law office was on the second floor. David Ficko photo.

7. Group of friends and family pictured in front of the Cole home Marysville, Ohio, circa 1904. Nellie Fairbanks is in the next to last row, midway, with a white chair back behind her head. Union County Ohio Historical Society.

8. Cole Family Gravestone, Oakdale Cemetery, Marysville, Ohio. Cornelia Cole Fairbanks's parents, two brothers, and

one sister are buried here. The small metal star indicates her brother Ulysses Cole's Civil War service. Author's photo.

9. Oil portrait of Cornelia Cole Fairbanks as a young matron in Indianapolis. Courtesy of Fairbanks Hospital, Indianapolis, Indiana. David Ficko photo.

10. Original Propylaeum Building. In 1888–89, Nellie Fairbanks served on the board of women who planned this notable expression of the late nineteenth-century women's movement. Bass Photo Co. Collection, INDIANA HISTORICAL SOCIETY.

11. Cornelia Cole Fairbanks, circa 1900. Union County Ohio Historical Society.

12. Mrs. Fairbanks delivers a speech at Jamestown, VA, 1905. Photo courtesy of NSDAR.

13. Mrs. Fairbanks and distinguished guests at the dedication of Memorial Continental Hall, 1905. Photo courtesy of NSDAR.

14. Memorial Continental Hall today. Photo courtesy of NSDAR.

15. The Fairbanks's Indianapolis home during the final year of Mrs. Fairbanks's life, the last building she planned. It now houses offices. David Ficko photo.

16. Nellie Fairbanks's grave, Crown Hill Cemetery, Indianapolis. The commemorative marker was placed by the Cornelia Cole Fairbanks Chapter, NSDAR, 2007, on the one hundredth anniversary of the chapter's founding. David Ficko photo.

17. Fairbanks Monument, Crown Hill Cemetery, Indianapolis. David Ficko photo.

The face of the monument reads:

CHARLES WARREN FAIRBANKS
U. S. SENATE 1897–1905
VICE PRESIDENT THE
UNITED STATES 1905–1909

———————

CORNELIA COLE FAIRBANKS
PRESIDENT GENERAL
D. A. R.
1901–1905

Acknowledgements

Not long after I retired from the faculty of Indiana University School of Medicine, I became involved in the Fairbanks educational programs for addictions and mental health counselors throughout Indiana, part of the Fairbanks Hospital and outpatient addiction treatment services. Along the way, I became intrigued with the life of Cornelia Cole Fairbanks, for whom the hospital had been named. Betsy Bikoff, of the Richard M. Fairbanks Foundation, gave encouragement in my quest for information, as did Helene Cross, president and CEO of Fairbanks Hospital and addiction treatment programs.

The staffs of the William Henry Smith Library, Indiana Historical Society, Indianapolis; the Indiana State Library, Indianapolis; and the Lilly Manuscripts Library, Indiana University, Bloomington; were most helpful, as was Dr. Alan January at the Indiana Archives, Indianapolis. Ray Boomhower's article, "The Fatal Cocktail," in *TRACES of Indiana and Midwestern History* provided an invaluable resource about Vice President Fairbanks.

President General Linda Gist Calvin, National Society Daughters of the American Revolution, generously gave me permission to review relevant archives and photographs in the research archives of the society in Washington, D.C. I was greeted warmly there by Tracey Robinson, NSDAR Director of Archives and History. Assistant Archivist Rebecca Baird had researched all materials about Mrs. Fairbanks and collected them for my use. She and her assistant, Christina Lehman, were gracious and helpful with information and the provision of hard copies of materials I needed. Public Relations Director Bren Landon made photographs from the archives available to me.

Members of the Carolyn Scott Harrison Chapter NSDAR, Indianapolis generously made their chapter house library available. My erstwhile genealogy advisor and colleague Lynne Orvis continues to be a most helpful advisor about matters of the NSDAR.

As a matter of complete disclosure, I received the DAR Citizenship Award at Greenville High School, Bond County, Illinois in 1950. I must apologize to Mrs. Fairbanks posthumously that, although both sides of my family have Revolutionary War ancestors, none of us ever got around to documenting that sufficiently for membership in the Daughters.

Mrs. Pat Rooney introduced me to Linda Carlin, librarian at the Propylaeum Archives, another Indianapolis source of information relevant to the life of Nellie Fairbanks. David Ficko from the Fairbanks Hospital business office, a photographer of no mean repute, traveled to Marysville, Ohio, and around Indianapolis to photograph sites important in the life of Nellie Cole Fairbanks.

The resources of the Library of Congress in Washington and its very knowledgeable staff were, as usual, amazing. Their Pro-Quest computer database of historical newspapers from around the country was especially helpful. The *New York Times* online archive, 1851–1980 was also most useful, as was http://www.NewspaperARCHIVE.com/.

Courtesy and a love of history are alive and well in Union County, Ohio. Patricia O'Connor, Director of Special Collections, Marysville Public Library; Sue Kienbaum at the library; and Bruce "Bo" Johnstone at the Union County Historical Society in Marysville provided a great deal of information about the county's history and that of the Cole and Fairbanks families. The historical society provided several pictures of the Cole family. Records compiled by Margaret Main Bouic in Union County, Ohio, over many years are an amazing resource.

Kristine Kinzer, acting Serials Librarian and Curator, Ohio Wesleyan University Historical Collection, Delaware, Ohio, had researched materials about Cornelia Cole and Charles Fairbanks in response to my e-mails and provided further help and suggestions when I arrived there, as did Archivist Carol Holliger. The Ohio State Archives in Columbus had some information not available in Marysville and Delaware.

The Missouri Historical Society Library, St. Louis, provided knowledgeable staff and extensive resources related to the Louisiana Purchase Exposition of 1904 and the Republican National Convention of 1896. The St. Louis City Library, Main Branch, allowed access to newspaper microfilm not available at the historical society. The library of the Chicago Historical Society provided newspaper microfilm and databases relating to the Republican National Convention of 1904 where Charles Warren Fairbanks was nominated vice president.

Many friends and relatives gave encouragement and patient listening to my enthusiastic recounting of the latest cache of information I had found about Nellie Fairbanks. Jean Walker and Carol Tully provided insight as I was beginning the project.

My cousins Marietta and Richard Paterson, Champaign, Illinois, furnished a history of Piatt County where Charles Fairbanks owned 2,000 acres and built a summer home for his family. Marietta and Richard own a cabin in a pretty grove of trees in Piatt County where I have enjoyed many family gatherings. When I go there in the future, I will think of Nellie and Charley Fairbanks and their family vacationing a little over a century ago and not too far away.

My friends in St. Louis, Julia and Sally Watson and Sarah Boggs, regaled me with family stories of the Louisiana Purchase Exposition, helping me to better conceptualize this event and Mrs. Fairbanks's role in it. Julia, Sarah, and I had met while students at Washington University in St. Louis in the 1950s. I was aware that some of the newly constructed buildings at the university's present location had been used at the 1904 World's Fair, but little did I know that one of the buildings in which I had a number of classes a half century later had been the Women's Building at the fair. Some of the rooms had been the DAR Headquarters at the fair. Perhaps, even then, the ghost of Nellie Fairbanks was inspiring me. She could be pretty persuasive.

Printed in the United States
113850LV00003B/178-198/P

9 781434 385932